25 Steps to Power and Mastery over People

Other Books by the Author

25 Steps to Power and Mastery over People

James K. Van Fleet

PARKER PUBLISHING COMPANY, INC.
WEST NYACK, NEW YORK

Library of Congress Cataloging in Publication Data

Van Fleet, James K.
　25 steps to power and mastery over people.

　Includes index.
　1. Control (Psychology) 2. Success. I. Title
II. Title: Twenty-five steps to power and mastery over
people.
BF632.5.V35　　1983　　　158'.2　　　83-4208
ISBN 0-13-934810-7
ISBN 0-13-934802-6 {PBK}

This book is dedicated to my grandchildren who have filled my life with abundant joy and happiness:

Jessica Marie Van Fleet
Dara Nicole Van Fleet
Christina Lynne Van Fleet
Joel Van Spain
Adam Lucas Spain
Kelly Michelle Cook

What This Book Will Do for You

This book will show you how to master people and gain power over them. You will learn how to influence and control certain key individuals in your life so you can achieve your goals and become successful.

If you read and put into practice only one step a day, in only twenty-five days—less than a month—you'll be able to turn your life completely around. You'll develop the ability to gain remarkable and spectacular achievements instead of having to accept just ordinary and average results.

Instead of taking orders and doing whatever you're told to do, you'll find that you can soon take over the leadership role yourself and be in complete command. You can gain power, influence, and control over others and attain complete mastery over people.

Let me tell you now about some of the marvelous benefits that will be yours when you gain this power and mastery over others.

You can become a real leader of people; not merely a slick persuader or crafty manipulator. You can become a leader and get whatever you want, for virtually everything you ask for, others will now give you. You can also forget all that foolishness you've been taught about getting along with people, being a good guy, and all that nonsense. That's strictly for followers, not for leaders; not for masters of people. When you use the power techniques that I'll give you, you won't have to worry about getting along with people. They'll have to get along with you!

Maybe you've been forced to kowtow to certain individuals in the past, to pay homage to them, agree with them, do favors for them. Now you'll be able to break that hold and turn the tables on them with your new powers.

In just a few short days you'll achieve a degree of personal power greater than anything you've ever experienced before. Prestige, respect, influence—all these will now come your way. Don't be surprised when even previously unfriendly people approach you, actually want to be with you, want to do things for you. It will happen.

Even powerful people like your boss, stubborn customers and clients, intractable authorities, will recognize a new power in you and give in to your requests. With this new power you possess, you can be elected to the presidency and chairmanship of clubs and groups if that's what you desire. In fact, wherever you go, you'll be recognized and greeted as a powerful leader.

Not only will this book give you great personal power and mastery over others, but it will also bring about a tremendous change in you. Your true personality will emerge at last. When you look in the mirror, you'll see a completely new person; one who commands new talents, power, influence, and respect.

And that new magnetic personality will pay off for you at once. You'll be able to speak your mind about things where you've been hesitant to do so before. With the charismatic personality you now possess you can stand up before any group and put it under your complete control. Yes, you can become the leader of any neighborhood, religious, civic, fraternal, business, or political group you choose to.

Your new power can bring you innumerable financial benefits and rewards. People will start coming to you to offer you business deals, positions of leadership, perhaps even that big job or position you've been waiting for. The only limit is the one you place on yourself. Set your sights high enough and you can become president of your own company or hold down an important executive position in a corporation. You can become an outstanding financial success in the business world.

Now let me mention just a few of the techniques you'll find in this book that will help you achieve these terrific benefits for yourself.

In Chapter 1, you'll discover the fourteen secret motivators you can use to get people to do what you want them to do. When you use them properly, you'll gain complete mastery over others. The power that these secret motivators will give you to influence and control people is absolutely staggering.

In Chapter 2, you'll learn the three big secrets of getting people to pay attention to you and to what you want. Then, in Chapter 3, you'll discover the magic strategy you can use to build your self-confidence and, at the same time, win the confidence of others. In the next chapter, Chapter 4, I'll show you how to give commands and issue orders that will always be obeyed without question. Now that's real power!

In Chapter 5, you'll learn how to use the *Buffer Technique* that makes people support you 100 percent and back you to the hilt in whatever you do. Chapter 6 shows you a very valuable technique: how to ask others for money, and get it every single time.

In Chapter 7, you'll learn the secrets of how to govern people and control their actions with the words you use. The right language will truly work just like magic for you. Chapter 8 shows you how to develop the *Aura of Command* that makes others give way to you immediately. The methods and techniques you need to build an army of loyal followers will be found in Chapter 9, while in Chapter 10, you'll find the secrets of dealing with your listener's resistance and overcoming his objections.

Have you ever wished you could say just the right thing when you write a letter or a memo? Chapter 11 will show you how to write masterful letters that produce results every time. You'll also learn the *Power Words* that get your reader to take the action you want him to take.

An extremely interesting and worth-while subject is presented in Chapter 12: "How to Master and Control the Opposite Sex." Now who doesn't want to learn how to do that? This chapter will also show you how to use the *Steepling Technique* to project your power to others.

Did you ever want to know how to turn an enemy into a loyal and devoted friend whom you could trust? I'll show you how you can do that in Chapter 13. How often have you wanted to influence and control a person the first time you met, but weren't able to do so? You'll learn an amazing strategy in Chapter 14 that will let you master a total stranger immediately. Do you have trouble getting your family to do what you want them to do? Read Chapter 15 and you'll find the solution to your problems.

In Chapter 16, you'll learn the *White Magic* technique that turns off a person's anger immediately. You'll also learn the *Fact-Finder* technique to stop an angry person dead in his tracks and the

Power Play that quickly squelches an individual's anger.

Chapter 17 shows you how to master the art of getting ahead in today's business world. You'll be given the techniques that a secretary used to become the Chief Administrative Officer of a giant corporation. You'll also learn a clever technique that you can use to get yourself promoted to a top-level position.

Chapter 18 gives you a variety of techniques that enables you to handle other members of the *power elite*—and come out on top. For example, you'll learn how to create your own *Space Bubble* to protect your power base. And you'll be shown how you can use *Silent Power Cues* to project your personal charisma and magnetism.

Would you like to know how to handle problem people? In Chapter 19 you'll learn the *Secret Leverage* that makes the problem person like putty in your hands. Did you ever wonder how to master and control large groups of people? Chapter 20 will give you the techniques that great world leaders have used to achieve power.

Chapter 21 takes up an extremely interesting and profitable subject: "The Secret of Verbal Brainwashing." Chapter 22 shows you how to get a person to tell you his secrets without your even asking him to do so.

In Chapter 23, you'll see how you can join that *Inner Circle of Power* to become an influential leader in your community. Have you ever wanted to be the life of the party but didn't know how? Chapter 24 will show you exactly how you can be the center of attention at the party or other social gathering.

Finally, in Chapter 25, I'll show you how to consolidate your power position so you can hold and increase your mastery over people, day after day, month after month, year after year.

How do I know this program of *25 Steps to Power and Mastery over People* will work for you? Because it has already worked for thousands of others. Yes, it's true. Thousands of people have already achieved mastery over people with this powerful, yet virtually effortless, program of mine.

They were just common ordinary people at the start. But by the end of the program—after spending only a few minutes a day for just twenty-five days—in less than a month's time they became vastly more powerful than they ever believed possible before.

And if all these people could do it, then so can you.

Contents

You'll Gain Complete Power and Absolute Mastery over People • You'll Save Much Time, Energy, Even Money • You'll Be Able to Influence, Control and Gain Complete Power and Absolute Mastery over Everyone You Meet • You'll Become a Brand New Person with an Exciting and Powerful Personality • The Secret Motivators That Turn People On • How You Can Use These Secret Motivators to Your Own Advantage • A Sure-Fire Guaranteed Way to Find Out What a Person Really Wants • Why Accurate Information About What People Want Is So Important to You • How to Use This Valuable Information for Your Own Advantage • Three Examples of How to Use a Person's Secret Motivators for Your Own Benefit

Use These Three Keys to Gain People's Favorable Attention • Three Big Secrets of Getting People to Pay Attention to You • The Five Major Benefits Sales and Advertising People Use to Gain Attention • A Technique That Makes People Pay Attention to You • Nine Benefits You Can Gain by Using This Technique

You to the Hilt • How You Can Use Participatory Management in Your Own Home • Use the Buffer Technique and People Will Back You to the Hilt • How Helen Gets Her Boss to Back Her to the Hilt • How a Garage Mechanic Gets His Customers to Back Him to the Hilt

How to Ask for a Raise—and Get It! • The Importance of the Proper Timing of Your Request for a Raise • Getting a Loan from a Bank • How Karen G. Got Her Big Bank Loan • Dressing for the Big Occasion • Bargaining for a Lower Price and Winning • How to Charge a Big Fee for Your Services • Never Act Desperate for the Money • How to Keep the Other Person from Saying "No" to You • How to Make the Other Person Feel Guilty or Worried if He Even Thinks of Refusing You • How to Make Others Glad They Gave You the Money

Why Language Is the Magic Key to Mastering People • How to Be Forceful and Convincing When You Talk • Why Verbs of Movement Are the Voice of Command • How Abstract Verbs Destroy the Power and Force of What You Say • Another Way to Sound Forceful and Convincing When You Talk • A Third Way to Be Forceful and Convincing When You Talk • How to Be Forceful and Convincing When You Talk: Nine Guidelines • Why You Should Know Your Purpose Before You Speak • Use This Technique: It Guarantees Respect and Obedience from Others • Three Magic Words That Will Always Get Results for You • Other Magic Phrases That Will Work Wonders for You • Potent Magic Phrases That Get a Person to Open Up with You

How to Best Time Your Arrival for Your Own Benefit • How to make a Dramatic Entrance That Commands Attention • Other Techniques You Can Use to Be the Center of Attention • How to Overcome Your Shyness with People • How to Project Your Individuality at a Party • Still Other Methods You Can Use to Command Attention • A "Party Map" That Shows You Where to Stand for Maximum Power

Your Key to Total Victory Is Your Follow-Through • Remember How You Got Where You Are Today • How to Set Up a "Lifetime Power Plan" to Project Your Goals for Those Years Ahead • The One Character Trait You'll Need for the Long Haul • How to Get the Most Out of This Book

25 Steps to Power and Mastery over People

1

Finding the Secret Motivators That Turn People On

You want to be able to gain power with people and achieve mastery over them so you can control their attitudes and actions. Then you can enjoy the benefits of having them do what you want them to do.

I know for a fact that you want to do this for two reasons: first of all, you're reading this book; second, every person I've ever met has this same basic desire for power. The mastery of people is everyone's goal.

Getting along with others is an important part of your drive to gain mastery of people. The ability to make friends and get along with people is a must if you want to attain real power over them. But that in itself is not enough. Here's why:

Although the friendly handshake, the big smile, and the cheerful greeting are all important, they won't get you anywhere unless you know exactly what the other person wants.

You'll never gain your objectives or achieve your goals unless you stop thinking of what it is that you want from that person and concentrate entirely on what you can do for him.

To be able to do that, you must get inside a person's mind so you can find out what he really wants. You need to know what actually makes that other person tick. You'll want to discover the *secret motivators* that really turn him on. Only then will you be able to understand why he says what he says—why he does what he does.

You don't need to be a psychiatrist or a psychologist, nor do you need any sort of advanced degree to be able to understand human nature so you can discover the innermost secret needs and desires of others. The techniques you'll learn, not only in this chapter, but also in the rest of this book, are easy to understand, simple to use, and most important of all, you'll find that they really will work for you.

I can assure you of that, for I have spent my entire life studying applied psychology: why people say the things they say and why they do the things they do. Give me a few minutes to listen to another person talk, and I can tell you what he really wants out of life for himself even better than he can. With a bit of practice and experience you can soon do the same.

In the lectures and seminars that I give for company and corporation executives, management personnel, businessmen and businesswomen, I show how they can use this valuable information about a person's deep needs and desires to gain complete power with people and absolute mastery over them.

In recent years, realizing that I could help more people through writing than through seminars and lectures, I've published numerous books on this subject. A few of the titles that have been extremely popular with company executives and business people are *Guide to Managing People, Van Fleet's Master Guide for Managers*, and *The 22 Biggest Mistakes Managers Make and How to Correct Them*. Another book that has helped hundreds of thousands of people, no matter what they do for a living, is *Power with People*. All my books have been published by Parker Publishing Company, West Nyack, New York, 10994.

This book not only expands and amplifies the information in my lectures, seminars, and previous books, but it also presents the latest developments in the field of practical or applied psychology.

Mastery of people will give you such power over others that they will give you everything you want. You'll become a leader of people—not merely a persuader, not just a manipulator—but a leader, pure and simple. Everything you ask, others will now have to do for you. When you use the methods and techniques that I'll give you here...

YOU'LL GAIN THESE MAJOR BENEFITS FOR YOURSELF

You'll Gain Complete Power and Absolute Mastery over People

When you know and understand those secret motivators that cause people to do and say the things they do, when you learn their innermost needs and desires, and when you make every effort to help them get what they want, you'll gain complete power over people and absolute mastery of them that will work like magic for you. People will always do what you want them to do.

You'll Save Much Time, Energy, Even Money

Do you ever wonder why some individuals are so successful while others fail so miserably? Or why so many small business ventures fold only a year or so after starting? The answer is quite simple: *Those who failed didn't determine what people's needs were before they started.*

The most successful companies, corporations, and individuals find out what their customers want before they ever start. They don't waste time, energy, or money in guessing. They benefit by finding out specifically what a person's needs and desires are through psychological studies and marketing surveys.

You, too, can save a tremendous amount of time, energy, and even money by using the same basic procedures. But you won't need to conduct an expensive psychological study or marketing survey to find out what a person's secret needs and desires are.

Before you finish this chapter, you'll know the secret motivators that turn people on. You'll also learn how you can use these secret motivators to gain complete power with people and achieve absolute mastery over them.

You'll Be Able to Influence, Control, and Gain Complete Power and Absolute Mastery over Everyone You Meet

As you study human behavior to perfect your understanding and knowledge of people—as you discover why people say the things they say and why they act the way they do, and as you learn to analyze their words and actions to find out what their hidden secret motivators are—you'll find that your ability to influence and control every person with whom you come in contact continues to improve. Your success will be inevitable.

You'll Become a Brand New Person with an Exciting and Powerful Personality

You don't have to be subservient to get along with people. That's strictly for those who kowtow to others. In this book, you'll learn the *real power techniques* used by famous world leaders. Use them yourself and you won't have to bend over backward to get along with people. It will be up to them to get along with you.

This book will open the door to an amazing development—the emergence of a brand-new you. Your own true personality—repressed possibly for years—the real you whom you do not even yet know, will now begin to appear. This new person will be completely different in looks, manners, speech, poise, confidence, bearing, and most important of all, the ability to gain power and mastery over people. Yes, the future is bright; it's the start of a great new life for you.

This new personality of yours will begin to pay off at once. For example, you'll see how you will soon be able to speak your mind in a way that everyone wants to, but nobody has the courage to. You'll do many things that few people dare to do.

Even if you're having trouble with your marriage or having other romantic problems, you can now forget them. It will be possible for you to have the appeal of a movie or television star; the charming manners of a diplomat.

So take a good look at yourself in the mirror right now. Make it a farewell look. In only a few short weeks an entirely new person—an astonishingly more powerful and masterful person—is going to appear before your eyes.

If you read only one step a day, in less than a month you will gain power, influence, control, and mastery over people. It will take you a mere fifteen minutes or so every day to read each step, but this can work a near miracle for you.

TECHNIQUES YOU CAN USE TO GAIN POWER AND MASTERY OVER PEOPLE

First, I want to tell you about the fourteen secret motivators that make people do and say the things they do. Then I'll show you how to use these secret motivators to your own advantage.

The Secret Motivators That Turn People On

It is extremely easy to understand all human behavior when you realize that people do and say the things they do because they have certain deep needs and desires that must be fulfilled.

Everything a person says and does is aimed at achieving those basic needs and desires. Some of these motivators are purely physical. Others are acquired through the learning process as one goes through life.

Physical Needs

The satisfaction of a physical need can become a specific goal that causes a person to behave in a certain way. Those basic needs are the ones that have to do with a person's physical existence and survival: food, drink, sleep, clothing, shelter, sexual gratification, and other normal body functions.

You will seldom have the opportunity to exploit or use a person's physical needs to gain mastery over him unless that basic need of his becomes an obsessive want because of greed.

Greed at times motivates all of us. Greed will make a person want a larger house than he needs, a more expensive car than he requires, better clothes, better food, and so on.

When a person's need becomes a want, it is also because he is driven by a deep learned desire, ego gratification—a feeling of importance and pride—plus a desire for more money and all the things that money will buy.

Don't misunderstand me. I'm not putting down money or the good material things in life. I'm only saying that when a person's requirement for these basic fundamental needs becomes a burning, driving, overpowering obsession to get more of them than he can ever use, it is because of greed.

You can always use a person's greed to your own advantage to gain complete power and absolute mastery over him. All you need remember is this: *When all other human motives fail, you can always appeal to a person's greed to get your own way.*

Desires or Learned Needs

Desires or learned needs are acquired by a person throughout his life as he discovers what is valued by other people and the importance of certain social attitudes and ideas. Psychological needs such as the desire for power, approval, recognition, ego gratification, liberty and freedom can be even stronger than the basic physical ones. People will do whatever is necessary to achieve them, be their methods legal or illegal, moral or immoral.

The basic desires or learned needs that every normal person has are these:

1. A sense of personal power, the mastery of others
2. Ego gratification, a feeling of importance
3. Financial success, money and all the things money will buy
4. Recognition of efforts, reassurance of worth
5. Social or group approval, acceptance by one's peers
6. The desire to win, the desire to be first, to excel, to be the best
7. A sense of roots, belonging somewhere
8. The opportunity for creative expression
9. The accomplishment or achievement of something worthwhile
10. New experiences
11. Liberty and freedom, privacy from intrusion
12. A sense of self-esteem, dignity, and self-respect
13. Love in all its forms
14. Emotional security

I have not listed these basic desires or learned needs in any particular order of importance. The point is, a person will not be completely happy and content if any one of them is not being satisfactorily fulfilled. Everything an individual does is directed toward their fulfillment. Every waking moment—every thought, word, and act—is aimed at achieving these goals.

How You Can Use These Secret Motivators to Your Own Advantage

It's up to you to find out which one or more of these desires is dominant in your subject. You'll need to discover which ones you can use to influence and control his actions so you can gain complete power and mastery over him. Find out what he wants above all else in life. Do that and you will be in complete command.

Although a person needs fulfillment of all fourteen of these basic desires, you'll soon discover that whatever a person is lacking at the moment, he has the greatest need and desire for.

By the same token, a surfeit of any of these basic needs or desires will prevent you from using it at this particular time to gain power and mastery over that person.

These two points may seem self-evident to you, yet I have often seen people try to gain power with an individual and mastery over him by fulfilling a desire that has already been satisfied.

Nothing is a bargain if it is not needed at the time. So, it will be up to you to find out which specific need or desire is most important to a person at that particular moment.

Remember also that a person's needs and desires are never static. They change constantly. What he wanted most of all a month or a week ago he may not want at all today. That's why you'll want to keep up-to-date and completely informed as to your subject's needs and desires.

A Sure-Fire Guaranteed Way to Find Out What a Person Really Wants

You have only one sure way to find out what a person really wants, and that is to ask questions. Of course, you can't be blunt about it; you must be subtle in your questioning techniques. You can use the following guidelines to draw a person out so he'll talk about himself and what he really wants.

1. Be genuinely interested in people, in each person and his problems.

2. Be a good listener. Watch for what he does *not* say as well as for what he says. Patience is necessary to be a good listener.

3. Encourage the person to talk about himself. Ask him questions to help him get started.

4. Always talk in terms of his interests so you can find out what *he* wants. Never tell the person what *you* want; he couldn't care less about that.

5. Make the other person feel important. Feed his ego and do it sincerely.

To get specific answers to your questions, use the five W's: *Who? What? When? Where? Why?* You can also use *How?* to get additional information about the person.

An insurance salesman, Bruce S., kept a record of hundreds of interviews to find out why people bought or failed to buy. He found that in more than sixty percent of cases, the objection raised against buying insurance was not the real reason at all.

Bruce found from his research that a person usually has two distinct reasons for doing anything: a reason that sounds good to his listener, and the real one that he keeps hidden all to himself.

Bruce recommends that to find the real reason behind a person's words and actions, you should simply keep asking him, "Is there any other reason?" or "And in addition to that?"

Why Accurate Information About What People Want Is So Important to You

> To gain power with an individual and mastery over him, you must know without a doubt what he wants so you can help him get it. That's why accurate information about what a person desires is so important to you.

I can best illustrate this point by giving you a specific example with which I'm personally familiar. A certain electronics factory was having all sorts of personnel problems. Individual morale and organizational esprit de corps were both at rock bottom. Quality control was turning back nearly forty percent of production. Absenteeism was running twenty percent above normal. The company's profit margin was being squeezed down to nearly zero.

The company called in a management consulting firm to see if they could find out exactly what was wrong. The consulting firm, after talking to a number of employees, made up a questionnaire listing eight specific basic wants. They then asked all the employees to list those eight basic desires in their proper order of importance.

The consulting firm also asked the company executives and management personnel to rate these same items—not in the way they personally felt about them, but in the order they thought their employees would list them.

Shown below are those eight basic wants listed in the order of importance by the employees. Management's listing is shown on the right side of the chart in parentheses.

EMPLOYEE'S RATING	EIGHT BASIC WANTS OR DESIRES	MANAGEMENT'S RATING
1.	Credit and recognition for work done	(7)
2.	Interesting and worth-while work	(3)
3.	Fair pay with salary increases	(1)
4.	Attention and appreciation	(5)
5.	Promotion by merit, not seniority	(4)
6.	Counsel on personal problems	(8)
7.	Good physical working conditions	(6)
8.	Job security	(2)

As you can readily see, the emphasis that employees and employers placed on these eight items is not the same at all. When management placed its emphasis on what their employees wanted—rather than guessing what they wanted—the company's troubles stopped, almost overnight. That was more than seven years ago. Today, that company is one of the top ten manufacturers of electronic equipment in the United States, with markets all over the world.

A point well worth mentioning here is that the employees have no union representation. They do not want any, for management gives them everything they want. By doing that, the company gets everything it wants, too.

My specific reason for giving you this example here is to show you that you cannot gain power with an individual and achieve mastery over him until you know what he wants so you can help him get it. Find out what your subject wants most of all; don't guess or make unwarranted assumptions.

Remember, all this effort on your part works to your advantage, for when you help a person get what he wants, you'll be able to get what you want as well.

How to Use This Valuable Information for Your Own Advantage

To find out what a person wants and help him get it is not only the number one rule in gaining power and mastery over others, but it is also the number one rule in all human relationships.

Think about this for a moment. If you follow this basic rule, it will solve even your family problems for you, too. It can be used in every sort of activity in which people are engaged.

You see, there is only one sure way to gain complete power and mastery over a person so he will do what you want him to do every time. That is to find out exactly what he wants and then to make sure he gets it when he does as you ask him to do.

For instance, does he want recognition for a job well done? Then make sure he gets it; praise his work. To whom does this apply? To everyone, from a child in school to a housewife, an employee or an employer—even the president of the company.

Does the person want to feel important? Then pay attention to him. Make him important; feed his ego. Does he want a chance to do something really worth while? Offer him that opportunity; give him a challenging job to do. Does he want emotional security? Offer it to him in whatever way you can.

When you show a person how he can get what he wants most

of all by doing as you ask, you can be assured of one thing: *he will do exactly as you desire when he knows for sure he will always get what he wants.* In fact, he'll do everything necessary to get what he wants, even if he has to move heaven and earth to get it.

That being so, you'll know exactly what your subject's actions and reactions are going to be to what you ask. As long as you make sure he gets what he wants when he does as you wish, you can accurately predict what he's going to do every time. You won't have to guess. You can forecast his response to the letter. And that is real power; it is absolute mastery over people.

Three Examples of How to Use a Person's Secret Motivators for Your Own Benefit

1. How Barbara T.'s Marriage Was Saved

Barbara T.'s marriage of twenty years seemed headed for the divorce courts. She called me one day in tearful desperation to see if I could somehow help her.

"I don't know what to do," she said. "Bill just doesn't seem satisfied with me no matter what I do. In fact, it seems that everything I do is wrong. He doesn't like the way I keep house, the meals I cook, the way I dress; says I'm cold in bed. He's constantly picking at me and criticizing what I do.

"We went to see a marriage counselor, but that didn't help at all. Can you do anything for us, Jim? I don't like to bother you, but you're one of my closest friends, and I thought maybe with your experience in applied psychology you could think of something that would help. I really do love Bill and I can't bear the thought of losing him. Then there are the children to consider, too."

I asked Barbara if she knew or understood the fourteen basic desires that we all have. When she said she didn't, I asked her to come by my office so I could give her a list of them and explain how they worked.

The end result was that Barbara's marriage was saved. When she learned what her husband wanted most of all from her, and then made sure he got it, their marital problems vanished.

The same system will work for you, too, if you are having problems at home. Just remember the basic rule: *Find out what your spouse wants most of all and help him or her get it.* Again, that's the number one rule in all human relationships, including husbands and wives.

You might ask now what Barbara got out of this when she made sure her husband's deep desires were satisfied. Not only did she save her marriage and gain a much happier life, but she also got a new sports car, membership in a tennis club, an annual vacation to an exotic resort of *her* choice, and a lot of tender loving care from her husband. Not a bad exchange at all.

2. How Ted J. Quadrupled His Income with These Methods

My insurance agent, Ted J., was making an average living using the old-fashioned standard approach of plugging security for the family if the man of the house died.

His secretary, Patricia, who attended some of my lectures, suggested to Ted that he change his sales tactics to offer the prospect the opportunity to control and dominate his family, even after death, with the proper life insurance program.

Ted called me the other day to tell me how much his business had improved with his new methods. "When I offered a man only security for his family, I was offering him a benefit he could never use himself," Ted said. "In fact, I was making him think only of his death with that kind of sales pitch and he just couldn't accept that idea.

"But by offering him the chance to *control and dominate, guide and direct* his family's activities even after he was gone, he saw that he was in a sense still alive. He was not completely wiped out of the picture. My life insurance sales have quadrupled with this new approach, thanks to you and my secretary."

3. How Jerry Increased His Air Conditioning Sales in Spite of the Energy Crunch

My neighbor, Jerry West, found sales lagging after the energy crunch that began back in the early seventies. People were willing to give up the physical comfort of air conditioning because of the high cost of electricity.

Jerry tried to figure out new customer benefits that he could use to stimulate his sagging sales, but he was at a loss as to how to do it. I pointed out to him that with open windows instead of air conditioning, homes were much more susceptible to burglary, so he should offer his prospects *safety and emotional security* as well as physical comfort and better health.

Jerry decided to try this new approach. To prove the point, he clipped police reports from our local newspaper and pasted them in a sales notebook to show prospective customers the rising crime rate in our community.

Then he would point out to his prospects that with air conditioning, the windows would be closed, the house would be protected, and the person could sleep peacefully all night long knowing that his family, his house, and his possessions were safe and secure.

"I've sold more air conditioning using your approach than I ever did before," Jerry told me. "Older people are more concerned with their safety than they are with their wallets, and we do have a lot of senior citizens here in Florida."

You can see from these three brief examples how others use the fourteen secret motivators we all have to gain power and mastery over people. Barbara, Ted, and Jerry found out what other people wanted and then showed them how to get it.

You may not be in business yourself, but after all, everyone's business is selling himself and his ideas to others to gain mastery and power over them. That's exactly what Barbara did and she isn't in business; she's a housewife. You can use this technique, too, no matter what your own individual situation is.

Now let's move on to the next chapter where you'll see how you can use these same secret motivators to get people to pay attention to you and to what you say.

2

How to Get People to Pay Attention to You

Perhaps your search for friends and companions is now being held in bondage because the people you know are unresponsive and won't pay attention to you. When you finish this chapter, those problems will no doubt vanish. About the only problem you'll have after putting the techniques in this chapter into practice, will be handling all the people whose attention you will attract.

I'm sure there are things you'd like to speak up about at times. Perhaps you've been somewhat hesitant about doing so before now because people haven't paid any attention to you. After this chapter, you'll have what it takes to stand up before any group, a crowd, even a mob, and not only gain their attention, but also put them under your control. You will be the master of any given situation.

With your new attention-getting techniques, you can be a leader—neighborhood, religious, civic, fraternal, business, political, family, or of any group you might want to influence and control.

Use These Three Keys to Gain People's Favorable Attention

To gain power and mastery over people so you can influence and control their actions, you must get them to give you their full and undivided attention. Only by gaining people's favorable attention can you get them to do what you want them to do.

You can do this by first arousing a person's *interest* and then fanning the flames of *desire* so high that he will have no choice but to take the *action* you want him to take. This is exactly what clever advertising and smart sales people do.

You may not be in sales or advertising yourself, but whether you are or not really doesn't matter. You're still in the business of promoting yourself and selling your ideas to others so you can gain power and mastery over them, be those other persons your friends and associates, your employees, or even your own boss.

As you develop your skills in gaining people's attention...

YOU'LL GAIN THESE WORTH-WHILE BENEFITS

1. You'll have no trouble at all in persuading a person to accept your idea, proposition, or point of view.

2. You'll be able to sell an individual easily on your product or service or on just doing what you want him to do.

3. A winning, positive, and outgoing personality will be yours. As your skills in getting people to pay attention to you improve, your confidence in yourself and in your own abilities will increase.

4. You'll be able to get others to think and act favorably toward you. You'll gain the power to master people so they will always do what you want them to do.

TECHNIQUES YOU CAN USE TO GAIN THESE VALUABLE BENEFITS

Three Big Secrets of Getting People to Pay Attention to You

Three big secrets of getting people to pay attention to you are these: (1) Know exactly *who* your listener is; (2) Find out *what he wants* most of all; (3) Determine precisely *how* you can help him get what he wants. I want to discuss each one of these techniques with you now in some detail.

1. Know Exactly Who Your Listener Is

If you were going to talk to a group of employees about increasing production or if you were conducting a meeting for sales personnel, I'm sure that your *slant,* your *emphasis,* and your entire *approach* would be much different than if you were going to brief your boss on the same subjects.

I'm not suggesting for a moment that you should talk *down* to your subordinates. Unfortunately, a lot of supervisors do that and then wonder why they don't get any cooperation from their people. So do many parents when they're disciplining their children. And some ministers talk down to their congregations just as many teachers do to their students. Frankly speaking, I know of no quicker and surer way to turn a person off than to talk to him as if he were inferior to you in some way.

Nor is it a good idea to talk *up* to your boss or to someone in authority, trying to polish the apple or gain favor with him. Flattery is as transparent as a see-through blouse, but not nearly as interesting. This is also a quick way to turn a person off.

To sum up this idea, let me say it is not wise to talk *down* or *up* to anyone. No matter who the person is or what he does, it's far better to talk *with* him. This is especially true when you want to gain power and mastery over that individual so he will always do what you want him to do.

Nevertheless, it is still true that the status, the position, the occupation of your listener—who he is and what he does—will most definitely influence the slant of your opening statement or your initial approach.

When you know exactly who your listener is going to be and what he's going to be like, then you'll want to...

2. Find Out What He Wants Most of All

In the first chapter I told you about the fourteen basic learned needs or desires that all people have. Just in case they've slipped your mind for the moment, let me sum up that idea for you here in one short simple sentence:

> Every normal person wants to know how to be loved—
> how to win money or fame or power—and how to stay healthy.

I also said it was up to you to *find out exactly what a person wants most of all so you can help him get it.*

How can you best do that? By paying complete attention to what he says to find out exactly what he wants or to discover what he needs. When you pay attention to a person this way, he will also pay attention to you. I guarantee it.

The reason for this is quite plain. You see, rich or poor, young or old, happy or unhappy, each one of us has a deep desire—yes, even a craving—for attention.

Let me give you a few quick examples of this. For instance, a crying child pulling at his mother's dress is demanding her attention. When she gives him the attention that he wants so much, he'll stop crying and behave.

What does the straying unfaithful husband want and need most of all? Ninety-five percent of the time he's seeking the attention his wife has not given him. When she gives the attention he needs, he'll stop wandering and stay home.

The nagging wife, the unfaithful husband, the runaway teenager, the rebellious child, the hypochondriac in the doctor's office, the patient on the psychiatrist's couch, the rioter in the streets, all these people are crying out: *Pay attention to me!*

Just look about you and you'll easily see for yourself plenty of examples of people demanding your attention, even in your own family. For instance, I have a granddaughter who wants to make absolutely certain I'm looking when she does something special for me. To make sure of my attention, Christina will look at me from the corner of her eye and say, "Now watch me do this. . .Grandpa, are you watching me?" And she's only three years old!

Remember that your listener is human, too. He also wants *your* attention, so give it to him. Pay attention to him and to what he says so you can find out what he wants, what he's most interested in.

When you give a person your undivided attention first, he will be forced to give his full attention back to you. He really has no other choice. Does this technique work? It most certainly does. It always has; it always will. It is a fail-safe procedure.

3. Determine Precisely How You Can Help Him Get What He Wants

After you know what your listener is most interested in, you'll want to analyze your own product, service, or offer to find out precisely how you can help him get it. Most of the time, you will already know how you can do that. All you need do is customize your approach to fit that person's specific needs.

For instance, people usually buy things for one of five reasons: *gain, safety, pride, convenience, love.* Just as a salesperson does, you should find out which one of these is the individual's main point of interest. That will be his most vulnerable spot on which you should then concentrate all your efforts.

Only by doing that will you be able to gain power and mastery over him. Let me give you an example so you can see exactly what I mean.

"A few years ago, I sold our house in town so I could buy a home in the country," Dave Andrews told me. "The saleswoman, Rachel Brown, couldn't understand why I wanted to sell our house in town for it was in an excellent location. It was conveniently located near a new shopping center and a school, yet not too close to suffer from any noise or traffic congestion.

"I explained to Rachel that when we first moved in we had a beautiful view of the little valley below from our front room window. But then a two-story house was built across the street, blocking our view.

"And in my back yard all I could see were my neighbor's garbage cans, his doghouse, a pile of bricks and scrap lumber, a compost bin, and a messy barbecue pit. As I told her, I wanted a good home with a decent view that I could enjoy.

"Well, Rachel had discovered my main point of interest—actually, weakness—so she concentrated on it from then on. She showed me a house in the country built high on a hill with a gorgeous view of the James River and the valley below.

"But when she told me the price, I laughed at her. 'Can't afford it,' I said. Rachel didn't argue with me. She just kept saying, 'Look at that view of the river—no one can ever build anything that will cut it off from you.'

"Every time I talked price, Rachel came back to the magnificent view of the James River and the valley through which it flowed. So what happened? I bought the house, of course! Actually, I bought the view of the river and the valley below. The house was just thrown in as an extra bonus.

"Rachel Brown was ever so smart. She really knew her business. She asked questions to get me to talk and she paid attention to what I said until she found out exactly what I wanted. Then she sold it to me!"

The Five Major Benefits Sales and Advertising People Use to Gain Attention

As I mentioned a few moments ago, people usually buy things for five different main reasons: *gain, safety, pride, convenience, love.* Although there may be some variations, these five major benefits are the main ones that smart sales and advertising people use all the time to gain a person's attention and interest.

I can almost hear you say, "But I'm not a salesperson. I can't use these benefits to get what I want the way they do."

You don't have to be a professional salesperson to use them. We are all salespeople no matter what we do. We all want to sell a person on our ideas so they will do what we want them to do.

For instance, you can use these sales techniques to sell your family on your ideas. You can promise your child a benefit for cleaning up his room, getting good grades in school; you can show your husband the advantages of taking you out to dinner, buying you that new dress, taking your vacation at the seashore instead of roughing it on a fishing or camping trip.

If you think you can't use any of these five major benefits that top sales and advertising people plug, then turn back to Chapter 1 and review the fourteen basic secret motivators that all people have. One of them is bound to do the job for you.

No matter what you do, you can use these sales techniques to gain a person's undivided attention. To learn even further how the experts use them, watch television advertising and you will see how these benefits to gain the viewer's attention are plugged over and over again. You'll constantly hear appeals like this on TV:

1. Takes less work.
2. It's easier.
3. New and improved.
4. Saves you time.
5. Does the job better.
6. Saves you money.
7. You'll be proud.
8. You'll look sexier.

A Technique That Makes People Pay Attention to You

You could try a variety of methods to get a person to pay attention to you. For instance, you could use a startling statement; an authoritative quotation; an unusual anecdote; a strong example. However, I prefer by far the use of the leading question that promises a benefit for it is without a doubt the most effective. Here are some examples of this potent technique:

1. How'd you like to make some easy money?
2. How'd you like to increase your profits twenty-five percent?
3. Want to meet a good-looking girl tonight?
4. How'd you like to cut your production costs in half?
5. Want to get rid of that tired, worn-out feeling?
6. How'd you like to be proud of your floors?
7. Want to get more MPG from your car?

No matter what your specific situation is, use the kind of question that promises your listener an immediate benefit just for listening to you; he'll be forced to pay attention.

Not only can you offer your listener a benefit with the leading question technique, but you can also get him to say "Yes" at once, and that's ever so important in gaining power and mastery over him.

You see, when he says "Yes" to your opening question, it establishes a positive mood. This makes it much easier for him to continue to agree with you.

Nine Benefits You Can Gain by Using This Technique

1. *With Leading Questions, You Can Control the Initiative in the Conversation.* You actually lead the other person's thinking in the path you want it to take. You point his mind in a specific direction so he'll give you the answer you want.

2. *Leading Questions Develop Your Listener's Interest.* A per-

son's attention span increases when you get him to talk by asking him leading questions. The more he talks, the more you learn about him and what he wants most of all.

3. *When You Ask Questions, You Stimulate a Person's Thinking.* Questions make your listener more alert and attentive to what you say. He becomes anxious to learn more. Many times, your idea becomes his idea and he wants to take credit for it.

I've seen managers and supervisors use questions to get what they wanted time and again by letting the other person think it was all his own idea.

4. *Questions Help Reveal Your Listener's Attitudes.* When you know what a person's thinking is and what his innermost feelings are, you can slant your approach to meet his individual needs and desires. You'll know which of the fourteen secret motivators you should stress to gain power and mastery over him.

5. *Questions Let You Know if You're Getting Your Point Across.* Attention is always lost when understanding is gone. One of the best ways to find out whether your listener understands you or not is to ask questions.

His answers will show you how good your methods and techniques are. At the same time, his answers will also indicate where your approach needs to be improved.

6. *You Can Reinforce and Emphasize Major Points of Interest.* Retention of major points of emphasis is made easier by frequent repetition. When you ask questions on a specific point, it is plain to see that you are stressing that idea. Your listener's answers will reinforce these major points of interest.

7. *Questions Give the Person a Feeling of Importance.* When you ask questions, you give a person a chance to express his opinions. That makes him feel important and fulfills one of his basic desires by feeding his ego. When he knows that you are interested in what he says, and that you respect his opinions and ideas, he'll respect your opinions and ideas, too.

8. *Questions Help a Person Recognize What He Actually Wants.* Remember Ted J., the insurance agent I told you about who quadrupled his sales by plugging the person's ability to control and dominate his family even after his death? Ted did that by helping

people recognize what they actually wanted from insurance. Help a person discover what he really wants most of all and you'll be in complete control. You will have complete power and mastery over him for he'll do whatever you ask him to do so he can get what he wants.

9. *To Find a Person's Most Vulnerable Point, Ask Questions.* Your listener's weak spot is your main key to success and complete power and mastery over him. When you know his most vulnerable point, don't hesitate. Attack! Concentrate on it; exploit it immediately. You can use it to get your own way without fail.

When you review this chapter on how to get people to pay attention to you, you will see that I have emphasized again and again the importance of asking leading questions to gain power and mastery over them.

But if you really want to know *who* your listener is—if you want to find out *what he wants* most of all—if you want to know exactly *how* you can help him get what he wants so that you, too, will benefit as well, you'll see that the only sure way to do this is to ask him questions, questions, and still more questions.

When you get in the habit of constantly asking questions instead of talking just to hear the sound of your own voice, you will find that the conversation flows more smoothly and that it's also much more stimulating and exciting. Not only that, you'll discover that it's profitable to you as well.

Asking leading questions that promise a benefit, then, is the surest way of getting a person to pay attention to you. Questions, rather than statements, can be the most effective way to make a sale, win a person over to your way of thinking, and gain complete power and mastery over him so he will always do exactly what you want him to do.

3

The Magic Strategy
That Wins People's
Confidence Every Time

After you finish this chapter, you will attain a degree of personal power and mastery over people greater than any you've ever experienced before. Prestige, respect, influence, all these will start to come to you now. Even formerly unfriendly people will approach you, actually want to be with you, work with you, do things for you.

You'll also discover that as your self-confidence increases, your power and mastery over people actually becomes self-generating. It will start multiplying of its own accord. People will come to you offering business deals, social honors, positions of leadership and respect, perhaps even the big job or position that you've always wanted.

However, before you can expect these good things to happen, *you must have confidence in dealing with people as well as confidence in yourself and in your own abilities to do your own particular job.* If either of these is lacking, you cannot possibly succeed.

I want to discuss these two important points first. Then I'll give you the specific techniques you can use to gain and hold a person's confidence.

1. Why a Person Lacks Confidence in Dealing with People

The main reason a person lacks confidence in dealing with others is that he does not understand why people do and say the things they do. He does not know what motivates people, what actually turns them on. He simply has not learned any of the reasons behind human behavior, including his own.

You can solve this problem quickly. To gain confidence in yourself and in your own abilities to master people, you'll first need to understand human nature and human behavior. When you know why people do and say the things they do, you'll find you have the answers to their questions and the solutions to their problems. You'll feel completely confident in dealing with people, and they will have full confidence in you.

That is precisely why I gave you that list of fourteen learned needs in Chapter 1, those *secret motivators* that turn people on. I recommend that you keep them always in mind, not only as you read the rest of this book, but also during every transaction you have with another person. You'll soon discover that your knowledge and use of them will work magic for you.

2. Why a Person Lacks Confidence in Himself and His Own Abilities

The reason a person lacks confidence in himself and his own abilities is that he lacks professional knowledge about the job. *There is no confidence killer more deadly than this one.*

Suppose, for example, you own an expensive European car and you take it to a mechanic who has worked only on American automobiles. He will be hesitant. He doesn't know exactly how or where to start. His every movement will show he has no confidence in himself and his abilities to repair your car.

But if you take your car to an experienced mechanic who knows and understands foreign automobiles, you will see that he goes about his work with complete confidence in himself. He knows exactly what he is doing.

The more a person knows about his own specialty, the more confidence he has in himself and his abilities to get the job done. There is absolutely no substitute for professional knowledge and expertise in building self-confidence.

BENEFITS YOU'LL GAIN WHEN YOU WIN PEOPLE'S CONFIDENCE

When People Trust You, They Will Follow Your Lead

When you show by your words and actions that you have absolute confidence in yourself and in your abilities to do the job, people—including your own boss—will trust you and have confidence in you.

If you are, or some day will be, a manager, foreman, or supervisor, remember that your people will follow your lead. They will adopt for themselves the same measure of confidence you show. Your confidence in their abilities will inspire them to use their full powers to get the job done for you.

You'll Be Able to Get Things Done

When you tackle a tough job with confidence and enthusiasm, you encourage others to do the same. You'll be able to get things done, for people work best with those in whom they have complete trust and confidence. In fact, when you show such confidence yourself, you can simply say, "This is what we have to do, here's how we're going to do it—now let's go to it!"

You'll Become Known as a "Can-Do" Person

When you get things done this way, you'll become known to your friends, associates and co-workers, and to your boss, as a "can-do" person. Can-do people have complete confidence in themselves and their own abilities. That's precisely why they become known as can-do persons.

Can-do people are always highly sought after in business and industry because they are so few in number. Freda Walker, the personnel director for a large cosmetics firm, says this about them:

> About the finest reputation men or women can make for themselves with us is to have it said that they always get the job done. They'll become known throughout the company as can-

do people. That's about the highest compliment they could receive, for it says everything we need to know.

But can-do people are not found only in business and industry. One of my neighbors down the street, Ellen H., a lady in her mid-sixties, is always active in Red Cross drives, civic betterment plans, and community affairs. She almost always assumes a leadership role in social activities because of her ability to organize a project and see it through to its successful completion. She is most definitely a can-do person.

So you see, you don't have to work for a company or corporation or be a big executive or manager to be a can-do person. You can use those abilities in your church, your club, or local social organization, just as my neighbor, Ellen H., does.

TECHNIQUES YOU CAN USE TO GAIN THESE BENEFITS

How to Develop Confidence in Yourself and in Your Own Abilities

If you lack self-confidence, other people will also lack confidence in you. So the first step in winning their confidence so you can gain power and mastery over them is to have confidence in yourself. How can you gain that self-confidence so you can win the confidence of others? One of the best ways is to *know your business and keep on knowing it*. In other words, you'll want to...

Be the Authority and Expert in Your Own Chosen Field

The person who knows his business, who is the authority and expert in his own field, has complete confidence in himself and his own abilities. This kind of confidence usually comes from extensive study, research, long experience, and plain hard work.

A certain physician I know, Dr. John M., an eye, ear, nose, and throat specialist, is sixty-seven years old. Yet he still spends four to six weeks every year attending lectures and clinics to keep himself up-to-date with the latest developments in his profession. Is it any wonder he is regarded as one of this country's top men in his field?

If you want to be the authority and expert in your own field, no matter what it is, you'll want to do the same. Don't stop studying just because you've graduated from school or have a degree. You'll never live long enough to know everything about your chosen profession.

Not only must you retain what you've already learned, but you must also keep up-to-date with new techniques and procedures so you can be ready for the future. No matter what you do, you'll need to keep on learning, for each day brings change.

If you want to retain your position as an authority and an expert in your own field so you can have confidence in yourself and hold the confidence of others, you should continue your professional education and development. There simply is no other way.

Use This Technique to Greatly Increase Your Self-Confidence

The other day I watched a young woman weight-lifter raise more than three times her own weight. Before she actually lifted those weights to win the championship and the gold medal, she sat in a corner of her dressing room all alone, eyes closed, talking to herself, psyching herself up for the task that lay ahead.

As I watched her preparation, a technique I have used for years came to mind for I knew she had to be using it, too. That technique is simply this: *Act as if it were impossible to fail.*

I know of no other method you can follow that will give you greater confidence in yourself. Never accept the possibility of failure or defeat in whatever you do. Don't misunderstand me. I do not mean that you should close your eyes to problems and obstacles that could keep you from reaching your goal. But if you will keep the idea of success uppermost in your mind, if you will always act as if it were impossible to fail, you'll find that solutions to your problems and ways to overcome your obstacles will soon come to your mind.

How Lloyd S. Uses This Technique to Achieve Success

A successful neighbor of mine, Lloyd S., says he never allows the possibility of failure to enter his mind. "I have complete confidence in myself and my own abilities," Lloyd says. "I have found from experience that a poor decision carried out with determination and force, vigor and enthusiasm, has a far better chance of succeeding than the best decision that is carried out in a careless and indifferent manner.

"Of course I make mistakes. Who doesn't? I wouldn't be human if I did not. But that means only that I've met with a temporary defeat; it doesn't mean I've lost everything. I never give up. I'll never fail as long as I keep trying. I will always succeed as long as I act as if it were impossible to fail."

Another Example of Why This Technique Works So Well

Our history books are filled with stories of famous people who became successful because they refused to quit. I'm sure you're familiar with most of them, but let me tell you about one you may not have heard. I learned about this one on a trip I made through the western states one year.

As I stood with other tourists staring in wide-eyed awe at the Grand Coulee, one of the world's largest dams, which is nearly a mile long and almost two football fields high, I wondered how it had been humanly possible to build such a tremendous structure. Then I heard the park guide say, "Had it not been for a young construction engineer who refused to accept defeat, the Grand Coulee Dam would never have been built.

"You see, the engineers working on the project had run up against a seemingly unsolvable problem. They had reached a point where their normal construction methods would not work because of deep deposits of constantly shifting sand and mud.

"Tons of it poured into newly excavated areas; it tore out pilings and scaffolding. All sorts of engineering techniques were tried without success. There seemed to be no possible answer to their problem and the situation began to look hopeless. In fact, some of the best engineering minds in the business were just about ready to give up building the dam.

"Then one of the young engineers had an inspiration. 'Let's drive pipes down through all that sand and mud,' he suggested. 'We can circulate a refrigerant through them and freeze the whole mess solid as a rock. When that's done, we won't have to worry about it coming down on top of us while we work.'

"So they tried his idea. In a short time, the unmanageable and shifting wet sand and mud had been frozen into one huge solid block. They could've built a skyscraper on it if they'd wanted to.

"The Grand Coulee Dam came into being and millions of people in the Pacific Northwest have benefited because one young engineer refused to accept defeat. Instead, he acted as if it were impossible to fail—and complete success was the end result."

So act as if it were impossible to fail yourself. You will be amazed at the fantastic results you get. Your self-confidence will grow until you know you can do anything you set your mind to. You'll become successful far beyond your wildest dreams.

How to Radiate Your Self-Confidence to Others

When you believe in yourself and your own abilities, your self-confidence will literally radiate from you. It will be reflected in everything you say and do. You'll glow all over with confidence and enthusiasm. And people are bound to have confidence in you, too. They can't help themselves.

What makes a successful doctor, lawyer, plumber, salesman? Confidence in himself and enthusiasm for what he's doing. Of course, the person has to know his stuff, he has to be the expert and authority in his own field, as I've already said, but unless he has confidence and enthusiasm, he can fall flat on his face. I've seen top students in school fail miserably in life while average students became rich and successful. I'm sure you've seen that, too.

It all has to do with confidence in yourself and enthusiasm for what you're doing. Let me give you two examples to show you, first, how a lack of confidence can cause failure, and second, how complete self-confidence can bring about success.

1. Why Even Smart Doctors Fail Sometimes

Even smart doctors sometimes fail because of a lack of confidence in themselves. "I can well remember when I had a low back problem several years ago," Lew Gordon told me. "Braces, plasters, and several weeks in traction at the hospital had done me no good at all. So I decided to see a chiropractor.

"This doctor was a smart man; no doubt about it. He had graduated from his college magna cum laude. A framed certificate in his office said so. He had also taken a number of postgraduate courses in chiropractic therapy as evidenced by the diplomas and certificates of attendance that I saw.

"But when I asked him if he could help me, he hesitated, and said, 'Well, I don't know...all depends on whether yours is a chiropractic case or not. But I'll try. Maybe a couple of treatments will do the trick, and then again, maybe not. I just don't know. I'm not sure. We'll just have to wait and see...'

"I left his office in disgust without getting an adjustment. This doctor had no confidence in himself and his own abilities, in spite of all his professional education and book learning, so neither did I.

"But my back still hurt so I had to do something. A friend of mine said, 'Why don't you see my chiropractor, Dr. Mary Bradley? She must be good; her office is always packed full.'

"Although I was somewhat reluctant to go to a woman chiropractor, I went to this doctor. After nearly three hours of waiting, I finally got in to see her. What a difference. It was immediately apparent. She radiated confidence in herself and her own abilities. She bubbled over with enthusiasm. She told me of the people she had helped, the ailments she had cured.

"When I told her about my problem and asked her if she thought she could help me, she stared at me in open-mouthed astonishment. 'Help you?' she asked. 'Of course, I can help you! What in the world do you think I'm here for, anyway?'

"Well, of course, I stayed. She cured my backache. How could she not have done so with the confident attitude she had?"

2. How You Can Inspire Others to Have Confidence in You

Let me tell you now about still another doctor I know whose confidence in himself inspires his patients to have complete trust and confidence in him, too. Dr. J. is one of the finest clinicians in the state of Florida. He has served as Chairman of the Department of Medicine at a famous Miami hospital for more than fifteen years.

The hospital administrator told me that the moment Dr. J. enters the sick room, the patient begins to improve. "The art of healing seems to surround his physical body like an aura," she said. "It is often not his treatment but his physical presence that actually cures the patient!"

What better example of how confidence in yourself and your own abilities can inspire others to have confidence in you is there than this?

If you, like Dr. J., can show by your every word and act that you are confident of complete success, no matter how hard that task might be, you will inspire others to feel the same way.

Such self-confidence develops the habit of success, even the legend of infallibility. With such a reputation, mastery over people will become a cinch for you.

How to Expand and Increase Your Power and Mastery over People

If you want people to believe in you, trust you, and have complete confidence in you, you must believe in them, trust them, and show full confidence in them first. It is a truism that like attracts like.

When you show this kind of confidence in people, you'll get far more cooperation from them. Give your people a vote of confidence. You'll be amazed at the extent of their capabilities when you show that you trust them to do the job.

This concept will work to solve all sorts of difficult problems. The more confidence you show in people, the more confidence they will have in themselves to do the job. You can then spend far less time, energy, and effort in supervision.

Show by your words and your actions that you trust people and that you have confidence in them and in their abilities. Your own power and mastery over people will be expanded and amplified as a result.

People will never follow your orders enthusiastically and willingly unless they have full and complete confidence in you. That's why this chapter had to come before the next one. It serves as the foundation stone for Chapter 4. "How to Give Commands That Will Always Be Obeyed."

4

How to Give Commands That Will Always Be Obeyed

When you know how to give commands that will always be obeyed, you'll truly gain great power and mastery over others. Such power will provide you with everything you want in life. When you can command people to do your bidding, others will have to do whatever you ask.

Even tough bosses, obstinate customers and clients, stubborn authorities, and anyone else who's been holding you back from attaining your goals of money and success will have to give in to you. When you know how to give commands that will always be obeyed, you'll get your own way every time.

If you want to get ahead in business or industry, if you want to succeed in your chosen profession, or if you want to be of service to your community, you must not only know how to work with people, but you must also be able to control and influence them so you can gain complete mastery over them.

One sure way of gaining this power and mastery over others is to be able to give clear and concise commands that are easy to understand. But issuing an order is not the end of it. You must know how to follow up and oversee its execution to insure it is promptly and properly carried out. In this chapter, you will learn how to do all that, and much, much more.

It could be that right now you don't have a job that requires you to supervise and manage people or give orders to anyone. I've had people tell me that when they actually did have such duties. If you will stop and think about it for a moment, I know you'll realize that...

There Will Be Times When You Must Give Orders to Someone

For instance, I can think of a lady I met who said, "I never give orders to anyone, I'm only a housewife." Yet a couple of hours later, Joyce was speaking to a group of people, telling them exactly what their duties would be in the annual United Fund drive. Her job? She was in charge of organizing and directing the collection effort for her city of 30,000. But she's just a housewife and never gives orders, or so she says.

Then there was Lucy, the cute little brunet nurse I met in the Orlando Medical Center when I went there to see my brand-new granddaughter, Dara Nicole. "I don't supervise anyone," Lucy told me. "All I do is see that the doctor's orders are carried out. Oh, excuse me for a moment. I want to say a few words to that new orderly. He never seems to get anything right.

"Bob, I told you to take the Smith boy's blood sample down to the lab immediately. They say they still don't have it. Where is it? And where are the tongue depressors and cotton swabs I told you to bring up from supply this morning. I wish you'd listen to what I tell you to do once in a while!"

See what I mean? So I'm inclined to doubt if you're in a position *never* to give orders to anyone. I know full well that if you are a father or mother with children at home, you have to give orders sometimes. Not only must you give orders, but you must also be especially adept and skilled in doing so with teenagers.

But if your job does happen to fall in that rare category of not giving orders to anyone, let me ask you this: What if you suddenly had to do so? What if you were put in charge of your group tomorrow? Would you know what to do? Could you handle it? Would you be able to give commands and issue orders that would always be obeyed without fail? When the time comes, you'll want to know how to get the results you want when you tell others what to do.

Learning how to issue powerful orders that will always be obeyed without question is a skill that can be developed. That's why this chapter is so vital to you in learning how to master people Before I cover the techniques you can use to develop this skill, first let me tell you about some advantages that will be yours when you give commands that will always be obeyed.

BENEFITS THAT YOU'LL GAIN

1. *People respond quickly to clear and concise orders and commands.* If you overstate your order by adding too many details, you can create confusion. The perfect example of the most concise and clear-cut order of all time can be found in Matthew 9:9 where Jesus simply said, "Follow me." And the Scripture says that "Matthew arose and followed Him."

2. *People work better when they know the results you want.* They will do a far better job for you when you tell them what their exact responsibilities are, precisely what you want done, and the specific results you expect.

3. *To decentralize the work effectively, issue orders that are easy to understand.* This is especially important in business and industry where a person always seems to need more time than is available. When people understand your order and know exactly what you want, you'll gain more time to do your own work and supervise the job that is to be done.

4. *You can get rid of waste, confusion, and duplication of effort.* When you use clear, concise, and simple orders, people will know what you want done and they'll do it right the first time around. Simplicity is an absolute must if you want to insure complete compliance with your commands.

TECHNIQUES YOU CAN USE TO GAIN THESE BENEFITS

How to Give Commands That Will Always Be Obeyed: The First Requirement

The first requirement in giving commands that will always be obeyed is to let a person know how he's going to benefit by carrying out your order. Before you give a person a command, forget completely what you expect to gain for yourself. Think the situation through thoroughly so you can tell him exactly how he will be rewarded by doing what you ask him to do. *Give him an incentive to obey your command.*

No matter what your order is, your listener always wants to know exactly what's in it for him. Let him know right away how he's going to benefit by doing as you say. This is especially true if you're going to tell a person how to correct a mistake he's making.

Of course, if he's working for you, he may have no other choice than to do as you say. But even if you're the boss, unless you stress the advantages the person is going to gain by doing what you want, he'll carry out your order grudgingly. You'll get only the bare minimum from him.

Even in the military, where a person has no choice other than to obey, explaining *why* an order must be carried out will mark the difference between a top-notch unit and a mediocre one.

So show a person how he can fulfill his basic needs and desires when he does as you say. It will be up to you to find out which secret motivator you can use to get him to follow your order to the letter.

When you find out what a person wants and then show him how he can get it by obeying your command, you can write your own ticket. You'll gain complete power and mastery over him so you can get the maximum results every time.

You can use these three techniques to set the stage so the person will be "in the mood" to obey your commands without question:

1. *Use Praise, Recognition of Efforts, Reassurance of Worth.* If you want a person to go all out for you, if you want him to follow your commands implicitly, praise him. Tell him what a terrific job he's doing, how much you need him, how you can't get along without him, how happy you are he's in your outfit.

Praise is the quickest and most reliable way to make a person feel important. It's also the least expensive, for it costs you absolutely nothing to praise a person's work. If you will remember, credit and recognition for their work was the number one desire of the electronics factory's employees in Chapter 1. If it worked for them, it'll work for you.

So give the person the praise he needs so much, the importance he craves, the credit and recognition he wants. He'll not only obey your commands without fail, he'll almost jump through hoops to get more of it.

2. *Make His Job Interesting and Worth-while.* Let a person know why his job is important and how it contributes to the success

of the entire group. When a person understands the purpose behind his job and the part it plays in the larger scheme of things, the greater the interest he will have in his work.

3. *Offer a Person Emotional Security.* If a person is in constant fear of losing his job, demotion, suspension, or a penalty of some sort, you can never get him to work at his full potential. You cannot use fear or threats and expect to get the best results. Fear leads to hate and when a person hates you, he'll never willingly obey your commands.

As an experiment, use these three simple techniques on your children. When you use praise instead of criticism, when you let them know how important they are to you, and when you offer your children love and emotional security instead of using fear and threats to get them to do what you want them to do, you'll be amazed at the cooperation you'll get from them.

How to Give Commands That Will Always Be Obeyed: The Second Requirement

The second requirement in giving commands that will always be obeyed is to *have respect for the dignity of every person.*

Never tell a person to do something that is degrading or embarrassing to him. Nor should you order a person to do something that you yourself would refuse to do.

If you treat a person with respect, he will return that respect with obedience. If you do not respect him, he will not respect you nor will he obey your commands. It's just that simple. Here is an example from my files:

Some years ago I was hired as a consultant by a tire and rubber company to help them solve their labor problems. Employee morale was at rock bottom. As a result of vandalism, some expensive major items of machinery had been wrecked and production had slowed to the point where the company was losing customers to its competition because it couldn't fill its orders on time. Pressure was on from the top to get things straightened out fast.

In just a few days, I traced their troubles to the mill department. All production began there. If the mill department faltered, every other section in the plant slowed down, too.

I soon found that the young mill foreman had no respect whatever for his employees even though he had been promoted from their ranks. On one occasion I heard him tell the night shift supervisor to "give someone a written reprimand and put it in his file. I want you to let those dirty SOB's know who's boss around here!"

Another time I stood with that young foreman watching the change of shifts in his department. It was just before 7:00 A.M., the official time for punching out on the clock.

The day shift had already reported. The men stood at their machines waiting to be told about the day's production. They needed only their supervisor's signal to start rolling.

The graveyard shift was exhausted; it was the end of their working day. Now that they were finished, they were squatting down on their haunches to rest, leaning against the iron safety railings around the heavy machinery, or sitting on stacks of rubber skids just waiting for the seven o'clock whistle to blow.

The young foreman called his outgoing shift supervisor over. "Get those men up and on their feet!" he snapped. "You know I don't allow those lazy bums to sit down while they're in my department. I'm not running a damned rest home here!"

"But my men are all through, Bart," the night supervisor protested. "You know we have a ten-minute changeover period. They're tired and simply waiting for the whistle to blow so they can punch out and go home. They're not actually working now."

"Don't talk back to me!" the foreman yelled. "I'm the boss in this department and don't you forget it. They're still on the clock so get 'em back on their feet. And that's an order, damn it!"

As you can readily imagine, morale in his department was the lowest in the entire plant; quality control was constantly turning back his production; the men hated him and there'd been all sorts of work slowdowns, even several cases of sabotage. I went to the plant superintendent with my report and my recommendation. I advised him to replace the foreman at once for it would be impossible to change the men's attitudes no matter how much he altered his own ways, and I had strong doubts if he could even do that.

The superintendent immediately replaced Bart with a new foreman. At the same time, he asked me to brief the new man and stay with him for a few days.

The new foreman saw the problem immediately. In a short time he had the department running smoothly again. Let me tell you exactly how he did that.

For the first two days, he simply walked around making no comment at all except to smile and say "Hello." The men, listless and discouraged from long mistreatment, eyed him suspiciously.

At the end of those two days, the new foreman assembled the department's personnel. He simply said, "I respect you and I ask for your respect in return." Little else was said and he took no other corrective action, but in less that forty-eight hours, the department was showing marked improvement and the rebellious men were once again doing their jobs and doing them properly. *All this because their new foreman had treated them with dignity and respect.*

There was also an interesting sequel to this. The plant superintendent had a seventeen year-old son who'd been in all sorts of trouble. He'd dropped out of school, been picked up by the police for possession of drugs on two occasions, arrested several times for petty theft and driving while intoxicated.

After seeing the results in his own plant, the superintendent realized that he, too, was guilty of treating his own son with contempt instead of dignity and respect. He changed his tactics completely and I'm happy to report that his son went back to school, graduated, and is now in college carrying a high B average.

What's the best way you can show respect for the dignity of every person, including your own children? Simple. Treat every man like a gentleman and every woman like a lady. Then you'll never go wrong.

A Technique You Can Use to Get Maximum Results from People

If you want to get the maximum results from a person, if you want him to do his best, then tell him *what* you want done and *when* you want it, but don't tell him *how* to do it. Let the person figure that out for himself. That way he'll be forced to use his own intelligence and initiative to get the job done. This is call a *mission-type order*.

Mission-type orders develop a sense of responsibility in people. Each person feels that he's really a contributing member of the team. No one is left sitting on the bench.

"Using mission-type orders can bring you all sorts of benefits," says Alberta Walters, a research worker with a Florida solar energy firm. "This is especially true in research and development. Our people have to use their imagination and ingenuity to come up with new ideas on how to get the job done. Whenever you use mission-type orders, you open the door wide for people so they can use their initiative to the utmost."

As Alberta says, mission-type orders will bring out the resourcefulness of your best people. If people are not stimulated to do a better job for you when you use this kind of order, they're probably not worth their pay at all.

A mission-type order is also one of the most effective ways to weed out inefficient and incompetent employees before they can become a burden. If a person can't handle it, he should be dropped and replaced with someone who can.

How can you use mission-type orders yourself? Easy. You can even use them in your own home. Instead of ordering your family around, use this technique, and you won't have to. Let your children you know what you want, when you want it, and then let them figure out how to do it themselves. This develops their initiative, their ingenuity, and teaches them to stand on their own two feet.

A Guaranteed Technique That Insures Compliance with Your Commands

Here's where so many people go wrong in issuing orders and commands, and why. *They do not supervise the execution of their orders.* Let me give you a typical example.

You issue an order. Everyone understands. You smile; you're happy. You figure you've done a good job. You go back to your office, sit down, have a cup of coffee, and read the morning paper. All's right with the world.

Meanwhile, everything's going smoothly. Your orders are being carried out promptly and properly. You might as well play a round of golf or go fishing this afternoon. Is all this true? No, it's not true at all! Why not? *Because an order without supervision is no order at all.* It's only wishful thinking.

To make sure the job gets done, and that your order is being followed to the letter, you must personally check the work yourself, for *a person does well only what the boss inspects*. Another way of saying this is *never inspected—always neglected*.

To inspect a person's work to make sure he's carrying out your orders without harassing him is an art. Over-supervision destroys individual initiative, but under-supervision is just as bad. A good way to supervise and not cause resentment is simply to walk around the work area and look wise. Your presence alone can act as a powerful stimulus to keep a person on his toes.

To see and be seen is a supervisory cliché, but it's true and it works, so you really ought to use that technique to make sure your orders are being properly carried out.

You can use this simple skeleton checklist to inspect and supervise to make sure people are following your orders:

1. *Set aside a specific amount of time each day for inspection and supervision*. Check some phase of your operation daily. Never let a day go by without inspecting something.

2. *Pick your inspection points before you inspect*. Pick at least three, but no more than eight, points to check at any one time. More than eight stretches your memory and span of attention too much. You must always be the expert and the authority; review these points first so you won't be caught short.

3. *Inspect only these selected points*. If you allow yourself to be led astray, you'll run the risk of exposing your ignorance. Remember that you're inspecting; you're not being inspected.

4. *Vary your supervisory routine*. Change things around constantly. Vary your times of inspection; change your points of inspection. Scramble everything like eggs. It keeps people on their toes at all times.

When and How to Use Suggestions and Requests Instead of Direct Orders

If your people have any initiative whatever, you can get even better results by using suggestions instead of direct orders. The average person doesn't respond well to direct commands unless he's in the service, and even that's no guarantee.

I have always been able to get extremely good results by *asking* a person to do something or by *suggesting* he try it a certain way.

There's no law that says you can't use expressions like "Why don't you try it this way? What's your idea on this? Would you be good enough to...I wish you would...Do you think you can...When could you have it done?" even when you're the boss.

One of the best ways to get a job done is to let the other fellow think it's all his own idea. Just plant your idea in his head in such a way that he'll come to think of it as being all his own.

This Final Technique Is an Absolute Must

Your oral orders must be repeated to you. *This is a rule*. Never violate it. When you do, you're sure to fail. If your subordinate does not repeat your order, it will almost always result in misunderstanding, mistakes, and hard feelings.

Sometimes people will balk at repeating your oral orders. They think you're insulting their intelligence. So be it. They will just have to feel that way. Don't worry; they'll get over it. They always do.

I've given you very few rules in this book. I personally believe in the use of skill, not rules, to get the job done. But this is one time I cannot back down. *Oral orders must always be repeated to you*. That is a rule.

If you will use the techniques I've given you in this chapter, you, too, can be a leader of people. There'll be no reason for you to argue with people, or to persuade them to do your bidding, or to try to manipulate or trick them into doing what you want them to do.

Just treat the individual with dignity and respect, let him know how he's going to benefit by obeying your command, use mission-type orders whenever possible, supervise the execution of your orders, and you will never fail. When you know how to give commands that will always be obeyed, you'll be able to get people to back you to the hilt, and that's the subject of the next chapter.

5

How to Get People to Back You to the Hilt

After only four chapters, the new personality you are developing will begin to pay off for you, for people will now back you to the hilt. Your personal magnetism will grow and multiply; your power and mastery over people will amplify and increase. And that great new charisma of yours can act like a tornado, drawing people to you with its incredible power. You'll find that people will not only agree with you, but they will actually go out of their way to help you do whatever it is that you want done.

People will back you to the hilt no matter who you are or what you do when you practice the techniques that you'll learn in this chapter. To give you the broadest aspect possible, I've included examples that will show you how to get people to cooperate and support you 100 percent when you are or might some day be the big boss. Then I'll discuss how you can get people—including your own superiors—to back you to the hilt when you're not the boss.

An important method you'll learn to use is the *buffer technique*. You can use it to get even the most stubborn and recalcitrant people to cooperate with you and support you 100 percent. You'll also learn methods you can use in your family relationships that will get your spouse and your children on your side. When you can get people to back you to the hilt this way...

YOU'LL GAIN THESE MAJOR BENEFITS FOR YOURSELF

1. People will respect you and have complete confidence in you.

2. They'll give you their willing obedience, loyal cooperation, and wholehearted support.

3. People will work with you with initiative, ingenuity, and enthusiasm.

4. They'll work together as a team with high spirit and resolve—with conviction, purpose, and direction toward a common goal.

5. People will feel they belong where they are.

6. They'll work just as hard as you do to get the job done.

TECHNIQUES YOU CAN USE
TO GAIN THESE MAJOR BENEFITS

How to Get People to Back You to the Hilt When You're the Boss

When you're the boss and need people to help you do the job, you can usually get things done in one of three ways:

1. *You Can Give a Person a Direct Order to Do Something.* Even if that person is your employee and has no other choice than to obey you, this is normally the least desirable of the three major methods available to you, for you will usually get only the minimum results.

2. *You Can Ask a Person to Help You Do the Work, Using Your Already Established Procedures.* This is better than the first method, but it still leaves a great deal to be desired. This technique is commonly called "cooperation," but that word can be grossly misleading. For instance, management always says it cooperates with labor. What this usually means is that management furnishes the methods while labor supplies only the muscle. But that's not real cooperation at all. That's only giving lip service to the idea.

3. *You Can Ask a Person for His Ideas on the Best Way to Get the Job Done.* This is by far the most desirable method to use. It is called *participatory management*. When you use it, you will gain a person's cooperation and support. He'll back you to the hilt in whatever you do.

Why the Participatory Management Technique Is So Effective

Participatory management is highly effective, for when you ask a person for his opinions and ideas on how to get the job done, you've made him feel important, and that's one of the fourteen secret motivators that turn people on.

Making people feel important is a powerful stimulant and incentive to productivity. As a friend of mine, Dick C., told me, "I was so flattered by having the company president ask for my opinion, I couldn't get my hat on my head for more than a week!"

Not only do you make a person feel important when you ask for his ideas and recommendations about how to do something, but you also satisfy these additional learned desires that he has:

1. Recognition of efforts, reassurance of worth
2. Social or group approval, acceptance by others
3. The desire to excel, to be the best
4. The feeling of belonging, of being a member of the team
5. The opportunity for creative expression
6. The accomplishment of something worth-while
7. A sense of personal power
8. A sense of self-esteem and self-respect
9. Emotional security

When you can do all this for a person just by asking for his ideas and opinions, you know that he will back you to the hilt in whatever you do.

How and Where You Can Use Participatory Management

Participatory management doesn't apply only to business or earning a living. It can be used in your entire life—in everything you do. You can use participatory management in your personal relationships, your church and social activities, civic groups, school and community affairs.

One of the best places to use it is in your family relationships.

Marriage counselors tell me the divorce rate is much lower with couples who use this technique.

I've also learned from educational authorities that teenagers coming from families that practice this method in the home cause fewer disciplinary problems for their teachers. They also get along better with their fellow students.

So what it all boils down to is this: You can best succeed in life—financially, professionally, and personally—by getting other people to back you to the hilt. And participatory management is the best way you can do that.

So if you do want to get to the top, then use this technique in everything you do. It's a real key to your success. Let me give you some examples of how others use this method successfully to achieve their goals of power and mastery over people.

A Specific Example of Participatory Management in Business

As Jimmy Durante always used to say, "Everybody wants to get into the act!" Employees are no different. They want to have some say in how things are done, too.

You can make them feel it's *their* company, department, or section by giving them a role in the planning, decision-making, formulation of rules and regulations, policies and procedures. You can use any number of ways to let people participate in the management process. Let me give you one of the best ones.

One of the biggest personnel problems in companies and corporations is that executives and administrators at the top make up *all* the rules and regulations for people at the bottom.

But most people—and that includes me, too—don't like being told what or what not to do. They rebel automatically. After all, rules and regulations are restrictions on their personal and individual liberties. So people tend to resist those rules or disobey them altogether.

If that's the problem in your group, let me suggest you use the method Jennifer Morton, a personnel manager, recommends. Here's what she says about how her company uses the participatory management technique to get results.

"One of the best ways we've found to cooperate with our employees is to let them make up their own rules and regulations to govern themselves," Jennifer says. "After all, no two departments have the same functions or identical tasks, so it's difficult for top management to work out rules that apply to everyone.

"Not only that, our boss has found that when employees are allowed to set up their own rules for their departments, they are usually a lot stricter on themselves than we are. And since those rules are their own, the ones they personally made up, they will be more likely to follow them than when management tells them what to do or what not to do. It's an excellent way of using participatory management and we like the results we get."

How You Can Use This Technique to Get Even Problem People to Back You to the Hilt

I, too, have found, just as Jennifer has, that one of the best ways to get people to cooperate with me, support me 100 percent, and back me to the hilt is to let them make up the rules and regulations to govern themselves. This is especially true with employees who cause constant disciplinary problems.

I specifically remember one fellow—an especially obstinate and unruly troublemaker—who was so amazed by my asking for his help and advice in establishing the policies and procedures for his department, that he become a completely changed person. Almost overnight he became a model employee and set the example of behavior for others to follow.

Do you know why? *Because he wanted to be important, he wanted recognition, he wanted others to pay attention to him.* By feeling important, he was also able to fulfill nine more of his basic learned desires, the ones that I mentioned earlier in this chapter.

When I gave him what he wanted so much, he went all out for me, gave me 110 percent, and backed me to the hilt. His actions paved the way for all the others to follow.

So, if you want your people to cooperate with you, support you, and back you to the hilt, make them feel important. Feed their egos. Give them the attention they crave so much. Ask for their opinions and suggestions, their recommendations and advice. Show them how and why you can't get along without them. Give them a role in the decision-making process.

When you use participatory management with your people this way, you, too, will receive the same big benefits that huge companies and corporations have gained.

How You Can Use Participatory Management in Your Own Home

As I mentioned previously, participatory management will work for you and your family as well as it does for business and industry. If you've found this technique to be useful in your job, rest assured it will work with your spouse and children, too.

Dr. Wanda Ellis, a local clinical psychologist and marriage counselor, tells me a lot of husbands are at fault in that they never tell their wives anything at all about their business, their work, or their plans for the future even though all these affect the entire family.

"They never give their wives a chance to make any sort of suggestion at all," Dr. Ellis says. "Yet they complain to me, saying their wives won't cooperate with them in saving money, economizing on household expenses, and so on. A lot of fathers say their children don't cooperate either, but they never ask them for their suggestions or ideas. They only order them around and tell them what to do or what not to do.

"I always recommend to my clients with family problems like this that the husband, wife, and children, too, sit down no less than once a month for a family conference. At this meeting, problems can be discussed, common goals established, and each person can be asked to offer suggestions and recommendations.

"I am always deeply gratified when people with seemingly insoluble problems are able to resolve them when they adopt this family participative management plan. 'Impossible' situations are solved. The entire family gets along better. Everyone is much happier when each person is not told what to do or what not to do, but instead is asked for solutions to family problems."

I recommend this method wholeheartedly. Although our own children are grown and gone now, the family conference to get everbody's opinion and then vote on the problem has been our standard procedure for many years.

I always found that our children accepted parental authority more willingly, even when the decision went against them, when they had the chance to voice their own opinions and make suggestions before the final vote was taken.

I would also suggest that, as much as possible, you let your children make up their own rules of conduct to follow. I know that, just as employees do, they will obey their own rules and regulations better than the ones that parents lay down. Of course, they need your counsel and advice to help them, for after all, you are older, more experienced, and much wiser than they are.

Use the Buffer Technique and People Will Back You to the Hilt

The *buffer technique* is one of the best methods you can use to get people to back you to the hilt. Let me give you a specific example to show you how well it works.

A company controller, Frank R., was having all sorts of trouble with the people under him. Late payrolls were an especially sore point with him for they were a recurring problem.

When one of the department heads would take him to task for this, he would snap back testily, and say, "That's not my fault. I don't make up the blasted payrolls myself." He would then pass the blame down to one of his subordinates. That individual would then catch it from both Frank and the complaining department head.

"Frank, you're taking the wrong approach to solving this problem," I told him one day. "As long as you pass the blame down to someone else, you're going to have this difficulty. You are never going to solve your problem this way.

"But just as soon as you accept the responsibility for the mistakes of your subordinates and act as a buffer between them and those complaining department heads, you'll find that your people will back you to the hilt. They'll get the job done right and on time. If you protect them, they'll protect you."

Although Frank was doubtful about this solution to his problem, he decided to try it, more or less as a last resort. Naturally, this method worked just as I knew it would.

You see, I learned a long time ago that you must always accept complete responsibility and take the blame for the failure of those who work for you if you want them to support you 100 percent and back you to the hilt.

When you do that, you'll find that your people will go all out to keep mistakes from happening. *When you keep them out of trouble, you'll discover that they are anxious to keep you out of trouble, too.* The buffer technique, properly used, will help you increase your power and mastery over people tremendously.

The buffer technique should be used to help you accept the responsibility for the actions of your subordinates, not to cover up for them. For example, it would be a mistake on your part to use the buffer technique to hide an employee's alcoholism. You would only make his drinking problem worse by doing that. The best way you can help an alcoholic employee is to put him in touch with someone who understands alcoholism, say AA, for example.

How Helen Gets Her Boss to Back Her to the Hilt

Helen used to be known as a clerk typist. She now has the title of "clerical consultant," a nice fat pay raise, her own private office, and lots of privileges to go along with her title. And Helen's word around the office is absolute law. Her boss backs her to the hilt in whatever she says or does. Let me tell you how all this came about.

First, Helen is ambitious, smart, and assertive. She's anxious to get ahead. While typing letters, reports, and interoffice memos, she stored up a lot of valuable information in her head. Within a few months, she had amassed a wealth of knowledge about the company as well as the likes and dislikes of her superior.

While taking dictation from her boss, George, Helen would occasionally make a suggestion or a small recommendation. When she saw that he listened and even put some of her minor recommendations into effect, she subtly pushed for more power. One day, she mentioned to George that most of the department heads regarded their secretaries as office furniture and weren't getting the most from their abilities.

"Okay," George told her. "Form a committee of all the department secretaries and study the problem. Then give me some suggestions on how department heads can improve their operations."

George told me that Helen put together an excellent report. "She didn't pull any punches at all," he said. "Those secretaries came right out and said such things as 'Our bosses have to learn how to communicate better with us. They act as if we're dumb clerks who know only how to take dictation, type letters, answer the phone, and make coffee for them. If they'd ask for our opinions and recommendations once in a while, they'd find out we could do things a lot better around here than we're doing them now.'

"Of course, there was a lot more than that. I liked their ideas so much that I put almost all of their suggestions into practice immediately. And I promoted Helen to a position where she could properly use her administrative abilities. I also gave each secretary a raise along with a letter of commendation."

How a Garage Mechanic Gets His Customers to Back Him to the Hilt

When you move from one place to another, two people that you want to find immediately are a good doctor and an honest, reliable mechanic. After I moved to Florida, I found the doctor almost at once. But it took me several years to locate the garage mechanic that I could trust. Here's how that happened:

One morning my neighbor was having trouble with her car. "I can't get it out of second," she told me. "I suppose I'll end up paying several hundred dollars for a new transmission," she said as she drove off to the garage.

But less than an hour later she was back home and her car was in the driveway again. "Marcia, what happened?" I asked. "Is your car fixed already?"

"Oh, yes," she replied, laughing happily. "It was only a missing cotter pin. Dale fixed it for me for only three dollars!"

I could hardly believe what I'd heard. "Where is this place?" I asked. "I've been looking for a good garage and an honest mechanic ever since we moved down here."

"Well, take your car down to Carter's Garage on Palm Bay Road," Marcia said. "They know what they're doing and they won't cheat you."

Marcia was right. I've had my car worked on at Carter's Garage ever since then and that was several years ago. Dale Carter is so honest that he'll let you watch him work as long as you don't get in the way. No other garage will let you do that. He's never lost a customer in all the time he's been in business. Everyone recommends him without reservation. His customers all support him 100 percent and back him to the hilt.

Dale's business philosophy is quite simple and like a breath of fresh air in a cynical business world. "If I can't earn an honest living working on cars, I'll do something else," he says. "I don't need to cheat anyone to make money."

I couldn't agree more. And speaking of money, let's get right into the next chapter where you'll learn how you can ask others for money—and always get it!

6

How to Ask Others for Money— and Always Get It

In one of my earlier books, *Guide to Managing People,** I used one chapter to discuss the vital importance of prior planning. The actual title of that chapter was "Prior Planning Prevents Problems."

That same thought is applicable here. The time you most need to do some solid planning is when you're going after another person's money, be that money a loan, a raise, or any other transaction affecting a person's pocketbook. After all, a man's wallet is next to his heart. When you want to part him from some of it, you need to plan carefully, for it can often be tougher than a dentist pulling a stubborn wisdom tooth.

So leave nothing to chance. Be prepared for all eventualities. If you're going to ask your boss for a raise, or if you're going after a bank loan, plan every bit of your action in advance. Know exactly what you're going to do; precisely what you're going to say. Above all, know the kind of person you'll be dealing with, what he likes and dislikes, what his idiosyncrasies are. The more you know about the individual, the better your chances are for success.

Prior planning can prevent most problems, so think of all the reasons the person might refuse your request. Then you can be ready to refute them with reason and logic.

---

*James K. Van Fleet, *Guide to Managing People* (West Nyack, New York, Parker Publishing Company, Inc., 1968).

THE BIG BENEFIT YOU'LL GAIN

Your power and mastery over people will help you realize one of the basic desires we all have: *money and the things that money will buy*. Ever since the Phoenicians invented money several thousand years ago, acquiring as much of it as one could has been one of the primary aims of every person.

This chapter will help you fulfill that basic desire so you can gain even more of it, and that's a mighty big benefit.

TECHNIQUES YOU CAN USE TO GAIN THIS BIG BENEFIT

Use the techniques you'll learn here and you'll be able to put the tough supervisor, that stubborn customer, the obstinate civil authority, or anyone else who's been holding you back from big money and great success, in his place.

For example, when you know how to get that big raise you're entitled to, you can order that new wardrobe of the latest fashions and the other luxuries in life that you want. All these can be yours when you know how to use your great personal power to gain mastery over your boss and get that salary increase you deserve so much.

Since getting a raise is of deep interest and importance to every single one of us, I want to cover that subject first.

How to Ask for a Raise—and Get It!

Preparation for your raise begins long before you actually ask for it. I talked at length with a career management specialist who teaches people how to get ahead and be happier at their jobs. Her clients include corporate vice presidents, managers, supervisors, bankers, secretaries, and many others, all of whom pay her handsomely for her advice.

You're fortunate; you're going to get the same information free. Ms. Davis says there are six vital steps to be taken in preparation for your raise:

1. *Become the Authority in Your Chosen Field*. It is important, first of all, to know your business and keep on knowing it. Progress

is perpetual. If you don't keep up with developments in your profession, you'll soon be passed by for promotion. But at the same time, don't think you're indispensable. No one is. I have a friend who retired from the Air Force as a three-star general. He thought the service would fold up without him, but to his chagrin, it continued to do quite well.

2. *Establish a Cordial Working Relationship with Your Boss*. No manager or supervisor will go out of his way to give a raise or a promotion to a person he doesn't like. The average boss likes people who *praise him sincerely and make him feel important*.

Smart employees appreciate their bosses and show them that appreciation. You can do that, too, without polishing the apple or flattering him. The best way to praise a person is to compliment him for what he *does*, not for what he *is*. *Praise the act, not the person*.

3. *Blow Your Own Horn*. The idea, that if you just do a good job, promotion and raises will come automatically, is wrong. Every *boss expects people to do acceptable work without making mistakes*. But that alone is not enough. You must make yourself noticed by calling favorable attention to yourself.

Often your boss doesn't realize just how good you really are. Let him know that—without being obnoxious or overbearing about it—in the office, at a business lunch, at an office party or at some other social function.

It also helps to become well-known in your community, for this brings credit and recognition to your company. Don't be bashful. Speak to church groups or civic clubs in your field of expertise. Groups like these are always looking for good guest speakers who will contribute their time without a fee. Have them send press notices to local papers. Get your name in print whenever possible.

Do anything you can to keep your name uppermost in your superior's mind. This is precisely the way the most effective advertising works. As one executive told me, "The most important thing about advertising is repetition. It takes constant repetition to build a reputation. We don't care whether people remember exactly what we say *about* the product. We just want them to remember the *name* of it. That's enough."

4. *Don't Hesitate to Delegate the Work*. If you are in a

supervisory position, or some day will be, don't hesitate to delegate the work to your subordinates. Every time you let something go, you free yourself to accept additional responsibility.

Top managers always feel much more at ease when they know that a competent person is available to take care of new assignments and new developments. Be smart; let that person be you.

5. *Keep Your Superiors Informed and Up-to-Date.* Without constantly breathing down their necks, let them know that your assignment is under control and proceeding on schedule. This shows them you are a dependable person who's getting the job done.

6. *Psych Yourself Up for the Actual Raise Negotiation.* Don't be backward about this or sell yourself short. In our system we equate value with cost. Your value to your company has a direct relationship to how much you're being paid.

Let your boss know the benefits he will receive when he grants your raise. One of the biggest benefits he'll gain is retaining your valuable services.

But before you issue any ultimatums, be sure you have a concrete job offer elsewhere. As a far wiser man than I once said, "The biggest fool in the world is the person who quits one job before he has another."

The Importance of the Proper Timing of Your Request for a Raise

When going after a raise, you should know which day of the week would be best. Mondays and Fridays should usually be avoided. Mondays can be filled with the details of getting the place going again. On Friday everyone is trying to clear his desk as rapidly as possible, getting ready for the weekend.

I also know from personal experience that just after Christmas or during the month of April, when income tax is due, it is not wise to ask your boss for a raise.

After taking into consideration these negative factors, let's look at a positive one. I've found that the best time to nail your boss for a raise is just after you've done a really outstanding job on an extraordinarily difficult assignment, and *he tells you so himself.*

Praise for a job well done is much appreciated. It is one of the basic desires we all have, but you can't eat words alone. The object of working is to make money. The more of it you make, the more important you feel, and the better you can live.

If your boss won't come across with a raise right after you've done a bang-up job for him, it could be that he never will, so it might be time for you to move on to where your talents and efforts will be better appreciated, not only psychologically, but also financially as well.

Getting a Loan from a Bank

Two things are important to a bank when you're asking for a loan: credit ranking and collateral. But not all banks demand the same amount of collateral, nor do they all think the same way about credit ratings. Some are easier to do business with than others. Don't pick a tough adversary if you can deal with an easier one. Let me give you an example from my own personal experience.

Many years ago when I was first starting out in business, I needed ten thousand dollars. I had only two thousand. I needed eight more from the bank. My father-in-law, trying to pave the way for me, took me to his bank and introduced me to its president.

I could tell from the moment I walked in that bank that my chances were minimal. It had the atmosphere of a morgue. People spoke in whispers. The place had cold tile floors, clammy marble walls, and dim lights. Not even a chair could be found in the lobby to sit on. Sure enough, I didn't get the loan.

So I went on my own to another bank. This one was modern and progressive. The atmosphere was warm and comfortable. It had wall-to-wall carpeting, good lighting, and comfortable chairs. Soft pleasant background music could be heard. The cashiers were warm and friendly. So were the loan officers. All in all, it was a completely different kind of bank. I got the loan.

Choose your bank as carefully as you do your friends. Chances are, you'll be dealing with that bank all your life.

How Karen G. Got Her Big Bank Loan

Karen G. wanted to establish credit, because she eventually expected to open her own small clothing store for women. So she first borrowed $100 from the bank's small loan department. She did not use the money at all, for she wanted only to build her reputation as a reliable person who would be a good credit risk.

She then borrowed $200, next $500, then $1,000, and finally $2,000, all on a signature loan without collateral. Each loan was paid off in the proper time. The bank officials got used to seeing Karen come in and looked on her as a responsible person who kept her word and paid her debts.

The day came for Karen to make her move. The store she wanted was available and she needed $5,000 to buy it. But she had only a few hundred dollars herself. When she went to the bank, the chief loan officer was on his way to lunch—as Karen knew he would be—so he told his assistant to "take care of Karen—give her whatever she wants—she's one of our most reliable customers."

Twenty minutes later, Karen walked out of the bank with a certified check for $5,000 in her hand, borrowed without any collateral whatever. By prior planning and using her head, Karen was able to accomplish what a lot of men would never have had the courage to do.

Dressing for the Big Occasion

I am not going into the details of how to dress when you're going after a raise from the boss or a loan from the bank. How you dress will depend on the customs of the area where you live and what you do for a living. Cowboy boots might be all well and good in Texas, but completely out of place in Chicago or New York.

But no matter what you wear, don't overdress for the occasion. Let me give you an example of that. My father was a farmer. Most of the time he wore bib overalls while working.

When he went to the bank for a loan, he changed from those overalls into a well-tailored khaki shirt and good-looking tan whipcord trousers with a matching jacket. He was thus quite presentable as a farmer going to the bank for a loan.

Bargaining for a Lower Price and Winning

If you pay less than the other party asks, this in itself is the same as demanding money from others and getting it. Let me give you a personal example.

For a long time now, I have rented motel meeting rooms in which to give my lectures to corporate and company managers and executives, and to hold my seminars for business people.

Rcently, one of the motels, with whom I've done business for many years, told me that because of inflation, they were forced to double my rent for the conference room. I felt that this was entirely too much, inflation or not, and told them so.

When the motel manager refused to back down, I said, "Howard, I know your expenses have gone up; so have mine. I am willing to pay you a reasonable increase. But if you insist on doubling my rent, then I have no choice but to take my business elsewhere.

"If you will look at your books, you'll find that I've rented this conference room from you every other month for ten years now. Not only have you made money from me, but you've also realized a handsome profit from my clients who've rented rooms from you, eaten in your restaurant, and patronized your lounge. If you're willing to lose all that, just say the word."

We settled for a twenty percent increase rather than doubling my rent as Howard had first asked. *To save money by bargaining for a lower price and winning is the same as asking others for money—and getting it.*

How to Charge a Big Fee for Your Services

An extremely successful Wisconsin chiropractor charges a substantial fee several months in advance for his services. If people hesitate, he will say, "Am I to understand you don't want to get well?"

If the person still is reluctant to accept his services, Dr. C. doesn't argue. He simply stands up to indicate the consultation is over and says, "Your loss is much greater than mine." He then calls his secretary to come and get the person. He leaves the room immediately even before she arrives.

"The prospective patient is so surprised that he can hardly believe what has happened," Dr. C. says. "My action of dismissing him summarily makes the person desperate to become my patient.

"He thought that *he* would make the decision about accepting my services. But I've taken the initiative away from him by indicating that I don't even want him as a patient. People will almost always stop at my secretary's desk after leaving my consultation room, and leave a check for the full amount that I asked for."

Never Act Desperate for the Money

One of the most important aspects of asking others for money, and getting it, is your attitude. Always approach the other person with complete confidence that you're going to win. Make it appear that you do not really need the money at all. It's just that it would be more convenient for you to have it.

Some years ago, I built a large swimming pool and a screened patio. The cost was quite high and the pool builder suggested that we finance it rather than pay cash. "Borrow the money and get a life insurance policy with it," he said. "Then if something happens to you, the pool will be paid off. Your wife will still have the cash you would have paid me."

The bank he suggested to us offered a seven-year loan, but it was an "add-on" type of loan. In other words, the interest for the entire seven years was added to the principal even before the first payment was made.

That meant I would be paying the same amount of interest on the final payment as I would be on the first one. It also meant that the total amount of interest would be far greater than if it were based on the unpaid balance each month as is the average home mortgage.

That banker was so confident that we would accept his terms that he had the loan papers all ready for us to sign. When he pushed them across the desk to us I pushed them right back and said, "This loan is not a necessity. It is only a convenience because of the insurance. I will not accept an add-on loan. I will borrow the money from you only if the interest each month is based on the loan's unpaid balance." Then I got up as if to leave.

The banker was dumbfounded. The average person always accepted the bank's terms without question. He waited for just a moment and then said, "Very well. I'll have the new loan papers drawn up for you exactly as you want them."

How to Keep the Other Person from Saying "No" to You

This procedure will work like magic whenever paperwork is to be signed. If no contract is called for, make one up anyway.

Have the contract all ready with your prospect's name, address, the amount to be paid. Every single thing must be completed so all the individual needs to do is sign his name.

When the person starts telling you all the reasons that he cannot accept your proposition, don't argue with him. And don't fold up your tent and walk away. Just hand him your pen and point out the big "X" where his signature goes.

Do you think this method is too presumptuous? Well, it is not. You'll be glad to hear that I've never made anyone angry by using this procedure. The magic of this technique is that *you concentrate a person's mind on signing—not on refusing.*

You crowd out all the reasons he thinks he should not sign until his mind becomes filled with all the reasons he should. His thoughts tend always to be translated into positive action.

How to Make the Other Person Feel Guilty or Worried if He Even Thinks of Refusing You

Last summer I had hurricane shutters installed on our family room windows. When the salesman came, I told him that I was interested only in getting a cost estimate so I could compare his figures with those of two other companies.

He let me know at once that if he'd known that, he would not have driven over ninety miles to see me, for their product was the best and would definitely cost more. However, he said it would be well worth the difference.

Without saying it in so many words, he made me feel guilty that I had infringed upon his time and caused him such inconvenience! And I thought to myself, *this fellow has taken a page right out of one of my own books!*

Even so, my feathers were ruffled, and I told him that if he didn't care to give me an estimate, he could jolly well leave at once. But he said as long as he was here, he might as well measure the windows and give me an estimate just in case I decided to give them the job. Then he wouldn't have to make a second trip, again an inconvenience for him!

After he'd measured the windows, he sat down, compiled his figures, and the next thing I knew he was pushing a contract across the table for me to sign. He was using the same technique I've just described for you in the previous section. I laughed and said, "You and I must have gone to the same school."

"No, not exactly," he said, smiling. "I just study my wife's notes. She attended one of your seminars for secretaries several years ago, and I'm using the same techniques she learned from you!"

Needless to say, I bought my hurricane shutters from him.

How to Make Others Glad They Gave You the Money

Before you part company, stress again all the benefits the person is going to gain from doing business with you. The best business is repeat business. The one-time sale where you have to make a new customer each time is a tough business to be in.

Let me ask you this: After you've bought a new car, how many salesmen have ever contacted you again? I've bought a number of new cars in my life, and of all those salesmen, only one ever bothered to get in touch with me afterward. In fact, when I'd take my car to be serviced by the agency where I bought it, most salesmen would run and hide to avoid hearing a complaint from me.

Let me give you a little tip about doing business with people. *Never forget a customer—never let a customer forget you.* Another way of saying it is, *the best way to get new customers is to take care of the old ones.*

So, always leave the person with a good feeling toward you. You may have to come back to the same well more than once for a drink of water.

I've taken a little more space for this chapter than I usually do, but money is such an important subject, I felt that not to cover it completely would not be fair to you. After all, money is the name of the game to most of us.

7

Magic Words That Command Respect and Obedience

After more than thirty years as a consultant in business management and human relations, I have found that a person's success depends as much on the ability to talk as it does upon the professional and technical know-how to do the job.

All other things being equal, advancement and promotion invariably will go to the person who has mastered the art of self-expression, both in speaking and writing, while his colleague, who attaches little or no importance to what can be achieved with the use of language, will be marked for mediocrity or failure. The famous British statesman of the 19th century, Disraeli, summed up this idea succinctly when he said, "Men govern with words."

Why Language Is the Magic Key to Mastering People

A well-known psychologist made a detailed study of hundreds of successful men and women to determine the reasons for their success. She found that all these people had one thing in common: *their skill in using words*. She also discovered that *their earning power was closely linked to their word skills*. You, too, can expect your own earnings to increase when you improve your skills in the use of language to deal with people.

If you want to be a powerful person in your business and in your community, you must be able to master and control people. Since you cannot use force to do that, you must know how to use words that will command respect and obedience.

I can say without any hesitation whatever that *when you can command words to serve your thoughts and feelings, you are well on your way to commanding people to do your will and serve your purposes.*

Learn how to govern and control people with words and you'll be at home in any social environment. Walk into any group. You will be as much at ease as if you were with your own family. You can be the leader in all the social, business, political, and neighborhood matters in which you're involved. Yes, you can even be elected to the presidency and chairmanship of a club or group. In fact, wherever you go, you will be hailed as the leader and treated with respect and obedience.

To gain power and mastery over people, then, you should first master the language. And language is important, for if you will analyze your day, you'll find that at least seventy-five percent of it is spent in oral communication with someone: explaining, persuading, advising, ordering, influencing, asking and answering questions. In short, you'll spend most of your time putting your proposals across to others—including your own family—so you can gain power and mastery over people and get them to do what you want them to do.

The more capable you become in expressing yourself clearly and precisely to others so there will be absolutely no chance of misunderstanding, the more successful you will become in mastering people and controlling their actions. When you become skilled in this art of communication...

YOU'LL GAIN THESE EXTREMELY VALUABLE BENEFITS

1. You'll develop a winning and positive outgoing personality.
2. You'll have greater self-confidence, inner security, and peace of mind.
3. You'll gain the ability to think clearly and to express yourself precisely.
4. You'll develop the power to master others so they will do what you want them to do.
5. People will listen to you and get the job done right the first time.

6. Your boss will take notice of you and recognize your talents.

7. Promotion and advancement will come your way as a matter of course.

TECHNIQUES YOU CAN USE TO GAIN THESE WORTH-WHILE BENEFITS

How to Be Forceful and Convincing When You Talk

Force makes what you say powerful and convincing. It gives strength and vigor to what you say. Force creates movement and movement creates force. Force makes things happen; it brings life to your words.

How can you be forceful and convincing when you talk? Only one way. Use many short active one- and two-syllable verbs that denote actual physical movement. Verbs like this make what you say move and come to life. Nouns and abstract manufactured verbs do not. They are dead words.

Since the verb is the only word that brings what you say to life, the more simple active verbs you use, the more forceful and convincing your language will be. When you use such verbs as *break, come, cut, dig, drop, go, kick, pull, push, stir, shake, strike, tear, throw,* you bring life and movement to what you say. Physical verbs of movement act as a stimulus and motivate people to take the action you want them to take.

Why Verbs of Movement Are the Voice of Command

Remember the classic words of Jesus Christ when he said to Matthew, "Follow me"? These two simple but powerful words form the motto of the Infantry School at Fort Benning, Georgia, and have been used for years by United States Army infantry platoon leaders.

Listen, also, to the words of the Roman centurion when he said to Jesus, "...and I say to this man, *Go and he goeth;* and to another, *Come and he cometh;* and to my servant, *Do this, and he doeth it.*" (Matthew 9:9.) The italics are mine.

Note the force and movement contained in such simple verbs as *follow, go, come,* and *do.* The abstract verb does not exist that could carry the physical force and movement that these short active verbs do.

How Abstract Verbs Destroy the Power and Force of What You Say

Such abstract and passive verbs as *finalize, conceptualize, consummate, ameliorate, promulgate, disseminate, obfuscate* make your speech flabby and roundabout. They bore your listener and cause him to completely lose interest in what you are saying.

Most abstract verbs are made from nouns by adding *-ize* or *-ate.* You cannot possibly sound forceful and convincing or speak with power if you use abstract and passive verbs instead of the short simple active ones that denote physical movement.

The more simply a thing is said, the more powerfully it will influence your listener. Short simple words make for strong speaking as well as for powerful writing. Note how much more force is in the sentence, "Spread the word!" than in "Disseminate the information."

Another Way to Sound Forceful and Convincing When You Talk

A second way to sound forceful and convincing when you talk is to use personal words that refer specifically to people and that have a natural masculine or feminine gender; for example, *you, me, us, we, he, she, John, Mary, mailman, actress.*

Avoid at all costs such terms as "They said" or "They want." These two phrases are used constantly to pass the buck. They completely destroy the force and power of your sentence and reduce your effectiveness.

A Third Way to Be Forceful and Convincing When You Talk

An excellent way to be forceful and convincing when you talk is to give your listener only one idea at a time. When you come to the end of one idea, stop. Take a breath. Then go on to your next thought. Don't link one idea to the next with such connectives as *and, but, for, or, nor.* Too many ideas at once bewilder and confuse your listener.

How to Be Forceful and Convincing When You Talk: Nine Guidelines

1. Use small active one- and two-syllable verbs of *physical movement* for power and force.
2. Use adverbs to add to the meaning of verbs rather than adjectives to modify nouns.
3. Use small easy-to-understand words. It's the simple things that last longest and wear best.
4. Use personal words like *you, I, we, us.* Avoid evasive terms such as "They said" or "They want."
5. Give your listener only one idea at a time.
6. Be direct and specific. Use illustrations and examples.
7. Don't use vague and abstract words. They muddle your meaning and confuse your listener.
8. Don't talk down to your listener by using pompous and pretentious words.
9. Don't bluff or beat around the bush. If you don't know the answer, say so.

Although a great deal more could be said here about word usage, grammar, proper English, and the like, I feel the information just presented is sufficient to show you how to use words that will command respect and obedience, and, at the same time, make what you say powerful and convincing. After all, the purpose of this chapter is to show you how to gain power and mastery over people with words, not to become a grammarian.

However, for those of you who would like to pursue the subject further, I would suggest you read Chapter 4, "The Master Formula for Powerful and Persuasive Writing," and Chapter 5, "Why Top Managers Are Always Masters of the Art of Oral Communication," from my book, *Van Fleet's Master Guide for Managers.**

---

*James K. Van Fleet, *Van Fleet's Master Guide for Managers* (West Nyack, New York, Parker Publishing Company, 1978).

Why You Should Know Your Purpose Before You Speak

Meaningful conversation usually has only one of three major purposes: (1) *to order or direct some specific action;* (2) *to inform someone of something;* (3) *to persuade someone to do something.*

However, at times your conversation may have a dual purpose. If you're talking to an employee, you may want to *inform* him of a mistake he's making and then *direct* him to change his procedure. To your boss, your twofold purpose might be to *inform* him of some problem and then *persuade* him to accept your solution.

Whatever the reason for your conversation, know what it is and stick to it. Don't wander. Ask yourself, *What is my specific objective? What do I really want to accomplish?* If you know exactly what you want to gain, your conversation will be powerful and convincing, clear and to the point.

But if you're not really sure of what you want to get done, you'll find yourself talking all day long about the weather, the state of your health, the last World Series, politics, the economy, inflation, and then wondering at night why you didn't get any work done that day.

A top salesman knows better than most people how to talk effectively to get results. Such a person is Roy Kendall, who gave me the following seven guidelines. Roy uses them in all his business conversations. Since his income is in six figures, I have no doubt whatever about their value.

1. *Lay your foundation* by being properly prepared. Know your subject better than your listener.

2. *Talk at the level of your listener's understanding,* no matter how much you know. Don't try to impress him with your superior knowledge; you'll only depress him. An extensive vocabulary is better for catching than it is for pitching.

3. *Determine your specific objective.* Know the exact purpose of your conversation and stick to it. Don't wander around aimlessly, and don't let your listener take the initiative away from you.

4. *Emphasize your main points of interest.* Come back to them again and again until they are absolutely clear in your listener's mind. The average person retains only half of what he's been told.

5. *Make up a mental outline and follow it.* If need be, write your main points down on a card that you can hold in the palm of your hand and refer to.

6. *Don't stray from your outline.* When you know what your specific goal is, it's easy to go from Point A to Point B directly without making any detours.

7. *When you've achieved your objective, stop talking!* A poor salesman often loses a sale because he keeps on blabbering after the sale has been made. He gives the customer a chance to change his mind. *When you're through, quit!* Don't be like the preacher who always says more than he has to talk about.

Use This Technique: It Guarantees Respect and Obedience from Others

No matter what you talk about, your listener always wants to know right away what's in it for him. Let him know immediately the reward he'll get just for listening to you. This is especially important if you're going to tell a person how to correct a mistake that he's making. Tell him about the benefits he'll gain when he uses your method.

A person's primary concern is always how he's going to benefit by doing as you ask, so tell him that. Of course, if he's working for you, he may have no other choice than to do as you say, but without the proper stimulus and incentive, you'll get only the minimum results.

So let him know right away how he can fulfill his basic needs and desires when he does as you tell him to do. Then you'll always gain the maximum from him.

If you will think more about what your listener wants to hear than about what you want to say, you'll get the response you want from him.

Three Magic Words That Will Always Get Results for You

"I need you" are three small words that build up a person's ego and make him feel important. I must admit that I've had others use these three words on me with devastating effect more times than I care to admit. You see, I'm susceptible, too!

People always want to feel they are needed, no matter who they are or what they do. I have a neighbor, a retired pharmacist, who knows more about botany than most professional botanists do. I'm always asking him for advice about some plant or shrub or tree.

When Bill tells me what to do, I thank him and apologize for bothering him and taking up his time. "Bother, my eye," he says. "When you're retired, you begin to feel completely unnecessary and unwanted. It's good to feel needed again!"

If you want your wife to be happy that she married you, then let her know she is both wanted and needed; not only in words, but also in your actions. And this same philosophy applies to the wife as well, so let your husband know that you need and want him, too.

If you want to get better cooperation from your employees, let them know that you need them; tell them how important they are, how valuable their work is to you.

One of the smartest personnel managers I've ever met is Nancy Wilson. She says this to each employee she hires: "I have a favor to ask of you. Even though I'm a woman and ninety-five percent of the people I hire are men, the company gave me this job because I convinced them that I had good judgment in picking the right individuals to work for them. If it turns out that I'm wrong, I won't have this job for very long. So *I need you to help me* by proving to the big boss that I was right in hiring you. Will you help me do that?"

How good is Nancy's approach? She's had her job for more than six years now. That should be proof enough.

Other Magic Phrases That Will Work Wonders for You

Such phrases as "I am proud of you," "What is your opinion?" "If you please," "Thank you," are worth their weight in gold. They'll literally work wonders for you when you use them. Let me show you exactly what I mean:

Just a few minutes from where I live is a large supermarket. But I never go there anymore. Can you guess why? Because I've yet to hear the words, "Thank you," when I pay my bill at the register. The clerks are sour and surly and never smile. They act as if they're doing me a big favor by taking my money.

So now I drive nearly five miles to a different supermarket to do my shopping. There I'm met with a cheerful "Hi! How are you today?" And when I pay for my groceries, the clerk looks me straight in the eye and says, "Thank you very much, please come again," as if she really means it, and I'm sure that she does.

Potent Magic Phrases That Get a Person to Open Up with You

As I said in the beginning of this chapter, seventy-five percent of your day is spent in oral communication with others. But conversation is a two-way street. Part of your time must be spent in listening to the other person. Sometimes that person is reluctant to open up and talk with you. Here are three magic phrases that will help correct that problem quickly:

1. "And then what did you do?"
2. "And then what did you say?"
3. "Please tell me about it."

Does this technique work? It most certainly does. If you want to find out what's going on in your own organization, use these magic phrases yourself. Just say, "Please tell me all about it." Then sit back and listen to what is said with an open mind.

Do you want your employees to like you and do their best for you? Then let them talk to you about their personal problems, their worries, and their fears.

Do you want a person to level with you, to tell you the truth? Then give him the courtesy of listening to what he says.

Do you want your wife to like you as well as love you? Then listen to what she says with rapt attention. That's ever so important, especially if she's been cooped up in a house alone all day.

To listen carefully and attentively is one of the highest compliments you can pay a person. It's also one of the most subtle techniques you can use to gain power and mastery over people.

As I mentioned in the beginning of this chapter, *men govern with words*. But there is much more to it than that.

Not only do you need to learn how to use words to gain power and mastery over people, but you must also develop the "aura of command" that will make others give way to you immediately. The next chapter will show you exactly how to do that.

8

The "Aura of Command" That Makes Others Give Way to You Immediately

When you know how to use the "aura of command control" that I'll tell you about in this chapter, you won't have to worry about your education or the way you speak. This technique will let you act correctly in any social environment. You can walk into any group and immediately be the center of attention. Your manner and bearing will attract others to you. You'll feel as much at ease as if you were home with your own family.

You'll never run the risk of embarrassment or personal challenge when your new aura of command control is projecting your power and influence over others. It will transform you into an astonishingly powerful personality. You'll have an important new look, new mannerisms, masterful bearing, new charm, a whole new status in life. Sound like a miracle? Yes, but it can all be true when you develop your own *aura of command control.*

How Certain People Practice This Technique of Command Control

Certain individuals seem to have the knack of assuming command of a situation, no matter what it is. Why is this so? *Because such a person is used to accepting full responsibility for his actions.* He immediately takes charge even when he lacks the authority to do so. And since most people do not care to accept responsibility, especially for a bad situation, they are only too glad to defer to someone who takes over the position of leadership. Let me give you an example of this...

How This Man Made Others Defer to Him on Sight by His Actions

"An automobile accident had happened out in the country," Sandra told me. "Several cars had stopped to look, but no one tried to help. Then another car stopped and the man who got out took charge of the situation immediately.

"He first checked the occupants of both cars and found that the only person seriously hurt was a woman. Her face had been badly cut, one arm had been broken, she was bleeding, and in shock. Since this was the dead of winter and it was icy cold, shock was doubly dangerous.

"This man checked to make sure she had no spinal injuries that would keep her from being moved. Then he turned and gave a series of rapid-fire orders to the people standing around.

"'You, go in that house and call an ambulance and the highway patrol. You there, go with him. Bring back two blankets to cover her with and a sheet or anything we can use to immobilize her arm.

"'The two of you over there, go find something we can use to carry this woman into the house to get her out of this freezing weather. Get a folding cot, some boards, a door, anything that will support her weight.

"'You two, go down the road to the south and slow down traffic. You two go up the road to the north and do the same thing. We don't want another accident. The rest of you get in your cars and leave right now.'

"In only a few moments, where before there had been only confusion, there was now order and organization, all because one person had taken command of a bad situation. His manner and conduct were so positive and authoritative that no one questioned his orders or his right to give them. People jumped to obey his commands, for they were anxious to help. They just needed someone to lead the way and take the responsibility for making the decisions."

So that's the first thing to keep in mind when you are developing your own aura of command control. *If you have the courage to make decisions and then accept responsibility for your actions, you'll find that people will always defer to you.*

You will be surrounded by an aura of command and authority

that, even though invisible, is still so easily recognizable you can almost touch it. People will automatically look to you for leadership whenever a problem arises.

Leadership Is Not an Inborn Quality

Leadership is not an inborn quality; it can be developed. Leadership is an art. It can be learned just as any other art is learned—music, carpentry, painting, medicine, law, plumbing, engineering. When you learn the specific techniques of leadership and develop your ability to take charge of a bad situation, I can assure you that the aura of command control that projects and radiates from you will make others defer to you on sight.

YOU'LL ALSO GAIN THE FOLLOWING BENEFITS

1. People will *instantly* do what you tell them to do.
2. People will turn to you for advice and assistance.
3. You'll gain the reputation of being a "born leader."
4. Your power and mastery over people will increase tremendously.

TECHNIQUES YOU CAN USE TO GAIN THESE BENEFITS

How to Make People Look Up to You, Respect You, and Give Way to You Immediately

If you want people to look up to you, respect you, and give way to you, you must accept full responsibility for your actions, including your mistakes. When people know you're not going to pass the buck to them, you'll gain their willing obedience, their loyal cooperation, and their wholehearted support.

Here are six simple guidelines you can use to learn how to accept responsibility and develop yourself professionally in this art of gaining power and mastery over people.

1. Seize every opportunity that offers you increased responsibility.

2. Do every job you're given, large or small, to the best of your ability.

3. Accept honest criticism and admit your mistakes.

4. Stick to what you think is right; have the courage of your convictions.

5. Take full responsibility for the failures of those under you.

6. Assume complete responsibility for your own actions—for your failures as well as your successes.

How to Get People to *Beg* for Your Services

One of the best ways to develop your aura of command control so that others will give way to you immediately is to become a *master trouble-shooter*. A master trouble-shooter is always in demand and well paid for his services. Red Adair, the expert who's always called on when there's a stubborn oil well fire that no one else can handle, is without doubt the most famous trouble-shooter alive today.

How can you, too, become a skilled trouble-shooter and have people beg for your services? Simple. *Become an expert in solving their problems for them.* You'll never run out of work, for as long as there are people, there'll always be problems.

Here's a three-step problem-solving process that will work to correct any difficulty you might have, no matter what it is:

1. Identify the exact problem.

2. Make an estimate of the situation.

3. Take the necessary action to solve the problem.

1. Identify the Problem

It's usually easy enough to solve problems caused by computers or machinery. Technicians and repairmen can do that. But to solve the problems caused by people is something else again. That requires an expert skilled in human relations who understands people's motives, needs, and desires. Since the mastery of people is the primary purpose of this book, let's look at some of the problems they can cause you.

You should use only one standard to decide whether or not a person is a problem to you. *He has to be hurting your performance, your production, or your profit.* This standard can be applied not only to business and industry, but also to your personal life and community affairs such as a collection drive, church, club, or other social activity. You can determine this by asking yourself three simple questions. If you cannot answer *yes* to at least one of them, then that person is not your problem, no matter how much you might personally dislike him.

(1) *Does he underperform in his job?* Is his work below the accepted norm in quality or quantity? Does he produce fewer units in a day than he should? Does he generate excessive waste or have a high rejection rate from quality control? No matter what sort of work is involved, does the person in question fail *in some tangible way* to measure up to your reasonable standards?

(2) *Does he interfere with the work of others?* Do you always find this person at the bottom of a disturbance? Is he a chronic troublemaker? Does his inferior work keep another department or section from functioning properly? Does his failure to produce cause trouble for another worker or another section? If so, then he is a problem to you.

(3) *Does he cause harm to his own group?* If this person is part of a team or group, do other members of his work unit try to leave it? Do people refuse to transfer to his work group? Is he causing his own team members financial loss? If you can answer *yes* to any of these questions, you have a problem person on your hands. After you've identified your *specific problem,* then you'll need to...

2. Make an Estimate of the Situation

To make a logical and orderly estimate of the situation, use these four steps:

(1) *Determine the exact cause of your problem.* You need to know *why* and *how* the problem arose so you can correct the cause, not just treat the symptoms. Dig up all the facts that bear on this problem. The more you know about its cause, the better you will be able to solve it.

(2) *Determine the possible solutions.* After you've found the basic cause of your problem, consider the possible solutions for it. Don't rule out a solution on first examination. Even if it later proves unusable, a tentative solution may contain ideas of future value. The more possible solutions you consider, the better your final one is likely to be.

(3) *Evaluate the possible solutions.* When you've gathered together all the possible solutions, then compare one with the other. Don't let your personal preferences or prejudices influence you when you're evaluating suggestions from others. For instance, don't reject Brown's idea because he has bad breath or Smith's suggestion because you're envious that he has such a gorgeous-looking wife. Remember, too, if you jump to conclusions you can often create a more serious problem than the one you're trying to solve.

(4) *Pick the best solution.* A point well worth mentioning here, for it's often overlooked—even by experienced trouble-shooters— is that your solution can be a combination of two or more of the possible solutions you've considered. You might take part of Black's suggestion, part of White's, and come up with a "Gray" solution that will solve the problem for you perfectly.

3. Take the Appropriate Action to Solve the Problem

Here, you simply put the solution you've chosen into immediate effect. Don't hesitate and waver with indecision. Your hard work is finished. Take the proper action. Issue the necessary order to solve your problem.

One last point I want to mention here is this: A woman often makes the best trouble-shooter for she has an instinctive sixth sense that helps her anticipate a problem even before it happens.

She can smell trouble coming as easily as you and I might smell a skunk. This sixth sense is really the essence of the mastery of any art, so a woman's intuition can be most valuable indeed in solving problems.

Another Technique That Projects Your Aura of Command to Others

Making sound and timely decisions without hesitation is one of the best ways to project your aura of command control to others. People will trust you and have confidence in you. They'll be motivated to do their best for you.

By the same token, nothing destroys people's confidence in their supervisor or their leader faster than the inability to make a decision. The American philosopher, Walter Kaufmann, once said that most people suffer from "decidophobia"—the fear of making the wrong decision. There are three main reasons for this fear:

1. *The Need to Always Be Right.* Some people can't make up their minds about even such minor matters as which movie to see, which television program to watch, or where to go on a vacation, because they are too afraid of making a mistake. It is not that the decision is a matter of life or death. It's simply that the person can't stand being wrong.

2. *Mixing Objective Facts with Subjective Opinions.* Most decisions should be made on the basis of objective facts. Very few can be made on subjective feelings. When these two are not kept separate, it is hard to make a rational decision.

3. *The Fear of Permanent Commitment.* Some people feel that a decision is fixed and irrevocable. Not true. If you make a wrong decision, the simple solution is to make another decision to correct it.

Two Examples of Indecisiveness

1. When Mildred was sixteen, her parents gave her a yearly clothing allowance and told her she could make her own purchases. Mildred was delighted until she had to make her first buying decision. She became so worried about making the wrong choice and displeasing her parents that she ended up buying nothing and went back to her mother for help.

2. Doris decided to go back to work when her daughter entered junior high. She was offered three good jobs, but she couldn't decide which one to take. After two weeks of agonizing, she finally made up her mind, but by then it was too late. All three jobs had been filled.

Guidelines to Making the Right Decision

Developing decisiveness is a matter of practice and experience. To help you learn how to make the right decisions, follow these guidelines:

1. *Learn to be positive in all your actions.* Don't delay; don't beat around the bush.

2. *Get the facts, make up your mind,* and then issue your order with complete confidence.

3. *Give yourself a reasonable deadline* for making your deci-

sion. A specific deadline can force you to come to grips with the facts.

4. *Try to limit your choices.* If you are picking out a new carpet, for example, and you are confused by the wide number of choices available, narrow them down by looking at only three at a time and picking the best one. Then look at the next three and pick the best one, and so on. Then take the best ones you've already picked out and repeat this same process until eventually you will have only one left. You can use this same system to pick out your suits, shoes, dresses, ties, and so on.

5. *Recheck decisions* you have made to see if they were sound and timely.

6. *Analyze decisions made by others.* If you do not agree, determine if your reasons for disagreement are sound and logical.

7. *Broaden your viewpoint* by studying the actions of others so you can profit from their successes or their failures.

8. *Don't make major decisions on minor matters.* Save your real efforts for the big and important decisions. Don't give yourself a migraine headache trying to decide whether to have string beans or asparagus for dinner.

How to Look the Part of a Commanding and Powerful Personality

To have the look of power and command so that people will give way to you on sight, you need not be six feet tall or built like a professional athlete. I have seen tall strong men turn and run in combat while small short men stayed and fought the enemy with courage. Power comes from within.

Of course, there are certain physical characteristics you can develop that will suggest power: a steady unflinching gaze, a tone of voice that implies complete self-confidence, and above all, a solid presence that lets people know you are exactly where you ought to be.

Your external physical attributes are important in your drive to gain power and mastery over others, for even when you don't say a word, your hands, eyes, mouth, and body can give away how you really feel inside.

Hands can indicate fear and anxiety in a number of ways: fingers twitching or drumming the knees, clinging hands, palms wet and clammy, hands visibly nervous in smoking, clenched fists, hands gripping the arms of the chair until the knuckles turn white.

Eyes can reveal fear by shifting back and forth and by lots of blinking. The mouth shows fear when one bites and licks his lips or has a tightly clenched jaw. Holding the body stiff and rigid indicates a deep-seated anxiety. So does excessive perspiration, constant deep breathing, or sighing.

Your entire physical bearing is important in projecting your power to others. Your posture should be erect, your head held up, and your chest out. You should show alertness and vital energy in all your actions and movements.

If you have confidence in yourself and always act as if it were impossible to fail, people will gain strength from your example. Your appearance and manner then must depict confidence, sometimes even beyond what you actually feel. By controlling your voice and gestures, you can exert a firm and steadying influence over those around you.

People always have the highest regard for the boss who remains calm in the face of trouble. And, conversely, they look down on the one who panics at the first sign of something gone wrong.

You increase people's confidence when you can view a bad situation with patience and a cool calm presence of mind. By such a positive attitude, you seemingly take the burden on your own shoulders. You give them the feeling that there is a way out of the dilemma and that the problem can be solved.

People will have confidence in your strength, courage, and ability to set matters straight. You will not only project an aura of command control that makes them give way to you on sight, but you will also increase your power and mastery over them tremendously.

9

How to Build an Army
of Loyal Followers

If you want to build an army of loyal followers, you must be able to master people and control their actions. This chapter will show you how you can be the leader in all the business, political, social, and neighborhood activities in which you participate. You can be elected to the presidency and chairmanship of clubs and groups if you so desire. You'll also learn a technique that will motivate your own spouse to be your loyal follower.

Professional people, like doctors and lawyers, try to convert patients and clients into a permanent loyal army of followers. So do ministers and politicians. Business people, however, need to build two armies of loyal followers: (1) employees, (2) customers.

If you have a small operation with only a few employees, such as the garage mechanic I told you about earlier, your main efforts will be spent on building only one army of loyal followers: customers. You don't need to be a big company employing hundreds of people to be successful.

Since my experience lies primarily in business and industry rather than in politics, religion, medicine, or law, part of this chapter will be used to show you how to gain mastery over your subordinates and turn them into an army of loyal followers.

It could well be that at this moment you might not be in the position to concern yourself with building up an army of loyal followers, but when that day comes, as I'm sure it will, the information in this chapter will be of inestimable value to you.

Before I discuss the techniques you can use to build an army of loyal followers, I want to ask you a few questions that will help you better understand the reasons behind my methods.

Do you ever wonder why the military services are unable to retain their highly skilled people? Or why some companies have a constant turnover of their trained personnel? The answer is simple enough. *They do not fulfill the basic needs and desires of their people.*

How is it that such highly successful corporations as IBM, Procter & Gamble, Eastman Kodak, Xerox, G E, Penney, and many others are all able to retain the loyal services of their employees for a lifetime? Again, the answer is quite simple: *They do fulfill the needs and desires of their people.*

If you, then, want to build your own army of loyal followers, do exactly as these top companies and corporations do: *Fulfill a person's needs and desires so he will become your loyal follower.*

Let me emphasize one point here. Before you think the methods used by these big companies are not appropriate for you, let me say that none of them started out big. Every single one began as a small operation. I can remember when 3M was a small, insignificant company almost unknown outside of Minnesota. How did 3M and the rest of these people become so big and successful? *They made loyal followers out of both their employees and their customers by fulfilling their basic needs and desires.* You can use the same exact technique to become successful, too.

Now only will this technique work to make you more successful financially and help you gain power and mastery over others, but it will also work to make your home life happier. That alone makes this chapter valuable to you. If you want your spouse to be loyal and faithful to you, make sure you take care of his or her needs and desires. Then you'll never end up in divorce court wondering how or why you got there.

BENEFITS YOU'LL GAIN WHEN YOU BUILD AN ARMY OF LOYAL FOLLOWERS

1. You'll have people who'll stick by you when the going gets rough.
2. People will respect you, trust you, and have full confidence in you.
3. They'll give you their willing obedience, loyal cooperation, and wholehearted support.

4. They'll work together as a team with high spirit and morale—with conviction, purpose, and dedication toward a common goal.

5. You'll make people feel they belong where they are.

6. They'll work with initiative, ingenuity, and enthusiasm.

7. People will work just as hard as you do to get the job done.

TECHNIQUES YOU CAN USE TO GAIN THESE BENEFITS

Why Loyalty Must Begin with You

If you want people to be loyal to you, you must give them your loyalty first. If you have someone over you, as most of us have, you must set the example for your people to follow by being loyal to your own boss.

Some supervisors and middle-management people try to gain favor with their subordinates by constantly criticizing or making fun of their superiors. This action completely destroys the confidence and loyalty of their subordinates. To be an effective leader so you can gain power and mastery over others, you must be loyal to those above you as well as to those below you.

To develop this quality of loyalty that will give you power and mastery over others, follow these six guidelines:

1. Be quick to defend your subordinates from abuse.

2. Never give the slightest hint of disagreement with your superior's orders when relaying his instructions to your subordinates. If you do disagree with his orders, tell him, not them.

3. Do every task assigned to you to the best of your ability. This in itself shows your loyal support of your superior's orders.

4. Never discuss the personal problems of your people with others. If a person tells you something in confidence, respect that confidence.

5. Stand up for your people when they are unjustly accused.

6. Never criticize your superiors in front of your subordinates. You cannot expect loyalty from below if you are not loyal to those above.

How These Top Companies Built Their Own Loyal Armies of Followers

1. A top-line mobile home manufacturer, headquartered in Indiana, has more than forty manufacturing and assembly plants in strategic locations throughout the United States.

The company president took over that position when he was only in his mid-twenties. In only fifteen years he has increased annual sales volume from 9½ million dollars to more than 250 million dollars!

Employees never leave to go somewhere else. They are all completely loyal to the company. They do not depend on a union to get higher wages or other benefits for them. Their pay is based on how much *quality* work they can turn out in a day. Morale is high. Each plant has a long list of people waiting to get a job there even though the company is non-union.

The company builds its mobile homes to order and to individual specifications. Employees work until the day's quota—usually twenty to twenty-two mobile homes for each assembly plant—is filled. Only then do they quit for the day. But this doesn't necessarily mean a long day. Actually, it can mean a short one, for if they're fast, they can leave early.

Management doesn't have to browbeat employees to get them to work. Employees police their own ranks. Not only do they eliminate inefficient or lazy people, but they also get rid of those trying to take shortcuts and skip necessary production steps in an attempt to speed up the assembly process and make more money. Employees know that if quality falls off, they will lose the privilege of quitting early while still getting paid for a full day's work.

2. An Ohio company inaugurated a profit-sharing plan for employees back in the thirties when many businesses were going broke. The basic concept of the plan was extremely simple: *The more money employees made for the company, the more money they made for themselves*. The end result was that all employees worked harder, produced more, and used their initiative and ingenuity to figure out better ways of doing things.

Instead of concentrating on how to "get" something out of the company, the employees used their brains to think up new ways to make more money for the company, and thus, more money for themselves. In a very real way, everyone was now part of the management team. Some amazing things happened after that profit-sharing plan was put into effect.

(1) Ordinary, average, working men and women came up with ideas that would do credit to an inventive genius like Edison.

(2) Work slowdowns became a thing of the past. All employees knew that the company's ability to pay depended entirely upon their ability to produce.

(3) The company's sales volume in 1980 was $400,000,000, an increase of eighty times more than the $5,000,000 annual sales in the early 1930s before the profit-sharing plan was started.

(4) The cost of the manufactured product has been cut more than half in spite of continued increased costs of raw materials.

(5) Annual wages for all employees have increased 600 percent, not from union demands or cost of living increases, but solely from employees' productivity.

(6) Counting bonuses, all employees—including the janitor—now earn more than $20,000 each year.

The company never has to worry about not having loyal employees. A long line of people is waiting to be hired, but there is seldom an opening unless someone retires or dies. Employees never leave the firm for any other reason.

3. Employees of Japanese firms are especially loyal to their companies. As an assembly line worker for Sony says, "Working for Sony is like working for the family."

The same can be said for all Japanese companies, whether they make cars, motorcycles, cameras, calculators, radios, TVs or whatever. Going to work for a Japanese company is like getting married, except that it lasts much longer than most marriages do in America.

Employee loyalty to the company stems from the company's loyalty to its employees. Company management pays a great deal of attention to the needs and desires of each individual employee—financial security, need for recognition and status, a feeling of pride in one's work.

How Other Top Companies Fulfill Employees' Needs and Desires

Most top companies offer their people *emotional security* in one way or another. I'm sure you'll notice this as you read the following examples. You can do the same, whether you're running a big company or a small two- or three-employee business.

IBM boasts that for thirty-five years no one has ever been fired for economic reasons. The company always finds new jobs for displaced employees, retraining them if need be.

Procter & Gamble people feel that the products they make are better than anyone else's. They feel that they are engaged in extremely worth-while work. The high morale accounts for the legendary competitive enthusiasm of the company's sales force.

Eastman Kodak encourages initiative and ingenuity by giving financial rewards for usable ideas. For instance, one employee received nearly $7,000 for finding a way to reduce breakage of camera gears. Kodak also likes to promote from within. Not many people ever leave the company.

Xerox has an outstanding benefits plan that pays 100 percent of all hospital costs for employees and their families. There is no limit. They also pay all dental expenses for those visiting their dentist regularly for two years.

The 3M Company offers so many opportunities to its employees that one senior official said, "The company is like a big cake. All you need do is cut as big a slice as you can eat."

General Electric doesn't fuss much about the chain of command. If an employee has a piece of work to do, he finds the person he needs to work with and goes wherever necessary to get the job done. All he needs do is keep the right people informed.

Weyerhaeuser, the biggest wood products company in America, gives its employees the freedom to make their own decisions.

J. C. Penney's people seldom leave either. As one girls' clothing buyer said, "Penney takes care of its own. They back you to the hilt on your decisions. It's good to know your head isn't on the chopping block for every single thing you do."

How You Can Use Teamwork to Build an Army of Loyal Followers

When you train people as a team, you give each one a sense of being needed and wanted and a feeling that he belongs. One of the strongest psychological drives in a person is the desire to belong to and have identification with a group. Give him that identification he needs so much, and you'll motivate him to be loyal to you.

When a person knows that he's wanted, that his work is appreciated, when he knows his efforts are contributing to the achievement of a worth-while goal, he becomes proud of himself and proud of the group. He'll have a strong sense of team loyalty.

When you promote a strong sense of teamwork in people, they will have a feeling of pride and loyalty. When you can promote a feeling of strong pride and fierce loyalty in every person in your group, your job as a leader will be much easier. When the chips are down, when your people need to give their best efforts for you, they'll respond and support you as members of a well-trained and loyal team.

Train people to work together as a team and you'll be better able to reach your goal and accomplish your mission. Teamwork in a big organization is the key to successful accomplishment of the mission. Teamwork should be developed not only within departments, but also between and among them.

Teamwork starts at the top and bottom and goes in both directions simultaneously. To be totally effective, it must spread laterally as well. All your people must work together as one big team for the common good if you want to gain the maximum results.

Use This Technique and You'll Win Every Time

As you've already seen from the examples I've used, my experience lies mainly in business and industry. But I do want to give you another technique you can use to build an army of loyal followers, no matter who you are or what you do. Simply said, that technique is this:

Establish an *emotional rallying point* for people to gather around.

One of the best ways to get people to cooperate and work together is to give them a goal to attain or a cause to fight for. People will unite solidly behind you if you can establish an emotional rallying point. Let me give you several examples of some extremely difficult causes to rally people to.

1. I have never known of a popular war. If ever there was one, then World War II came close to being it. Why? Because the American people were given an emotional rallying point, not by their own leaders, but by the enemy.

Up through the 6th of December, 1941, the American people were wishy-washy and noncommittal about the war in Europe and Asia. They could not have cared less; they had no interest in foreign affairs. But, when the Japanese attacked Pearl Harbor on the 7th of December, 1941, people's attitudes changed immediately. No longer was the United States a disinterested bystander.

After the war was over, the Japanese high command said that attacking Pearl Harbor was their greatest mistake. "Our victory at Pearl Harbor was in reality our first defeat," a high-ranking Japanese admiral said. "Although it was a highly successful maneuver from a military point of view, for our attack crippled the powerful United States Pacific Fleet, it was our first in a series of mistakes in underestimating the will of the American people to fight. Pearl Harbor was the emotional rallying point for the United States in World War II. It marked the beginning of the end for Imperial Japan."

2. During that same war, the famous Japanese-American regiment, the 442nd was formed. It became known as the "Go for Broke" outfit. The men in the 442nd gave it their all. One battalion was called the Purple Heart Battalion because of its high number of casualties. It was one of the most decorated units in World War II.

These men not only had an emotional rallying point, but they also had a cause to fight for. They had to prove to all America that they were not Japanese, but loyal American citizens born of Japanese parents. And of course they did.

3. Back in the 1930s, a comparatively small religious movement (it had a total of a little over 200,000 members in the late 1970s) established an emotional rallying point for its members by erecting a large headquarters building in Independence, Missouri.

It was called the Auditorium. It seats thousands of people and was built primarily by small donations from members in the middle of the worst depression the United States has ever known.

But after it was completed, the church began to stagnate. Today, it does not even retain its natural increase. Why? Because when the Auditorium was finished, so were the people. They no longer had a tangible goal they could aim for. The church leadership failed to establish a new tangible emotional rallying point around which its members could be gathered.

This last example shows that when the goal you establish by your first emotional rallying point has been reached, you must immediately establish another one. Also, the goal should be tangible as was the Auditorium.

Intangible goals are impossible for the average person to visualize, for they are too vague and abstract. They do not inspire or stir a person to action. If you disregard either of these points, you are only inviting failure.

I did not say that it is easy to establish an emotional rallying point so you can build an army of loyal followers. It is not. But if you put your imagination, initiative, and ingenuity to work, it can be done. The results gained are well worth the efforts.

How to Motivate Your Spouse to Be Your Loyal Follower

Since I am a man, I can best approach this from a man's viewpoint. However, I know that the techniques that work to gain a wife's loyalty will also work on the husband. This much I can say with great conviction. *The best method you can use to insure your wife's loyalty is to go out of your way to fulfill every single one of her basic needs and desires.*

A great many wives are homemakers and spend the entire day in the house, cleaning, sweeping, dusting, washing clothes, and cooking, but they get no appreciation or recognition whatever from their husbands for what they do.

I know of no quicker way to find yourself in divorce court than to neglect your wife's needs and desires and take her for granted.

You don't have to send her flowers or candy every day to show her how much you appreciate her. My method will cost you absolutely nothing and it's even more effective. I know of a couple who have been happily married for forty years, and I know for a fact that this man doesn't give his wife any presents except on her birthday, their anniversary, and Christmas!

"What's your secret, Tom?" I asked him.

"Very simple, Jim," he said. "First of all, I pay attention to her. I always let her know by my actions that I'm aware that she's around. I still say 'please' and 'thank you' even after all these years. So does she; it sort of builds a mutual respect between us.

"I never get up from the table without saying, 'Thanks, honey, that was a terrific meal,' or 'Thanks a lot, dear; you're really a wonderful cook.' No wife ever gets tired of hearing that.

"Or when we pass each other in the house, I just reach out and touch her hand gently. Or I bring her a glass of water when she's sitting down watching TV in the evening. Or a cup of tea in the afternoon when she's sewing or knitting. What if she doesn't want it, you say? Are you kidding? She'll drink it anyway just to show her appreciation for my giving her my wholehearted attention."

Little things? Could be, but if you want to maintain a harmonious relationship with your wife and want her to be loyal to you, then give her your wholehearted attention and your loyalty, too.

Not only will she be faithful and loyal to you, but your other benefits will multiply, too. I guarantee you'll never want for a clean shirt, you'll never put on a pair of unpressed pants, and you'll never sit down to a cold supper. Your wife will love these little inconsequential extras, and she'll want to make sure you keep them coming.

So try it. You'll like it, and so will your wife. PS: Mine does!

10

The Secret of Dealing with Resistance and Overcoming Objections

When you add the secret of dealing with resistance and overcoming objections to your arsenal of techniques for mastering people, you'll discover you're well on your way to becoming a powerful personality.

Perhaps you haven't realized yet the progress you've actually made, so just take a look at yourself in the mirror. You'll recognize that innate power, that inner aura of command that makes others yield to you. You'll see that you are becoming a completely different person, one who commands new talents, powers, influence and respect—a person who gets everything he or she wants. All the things you've always wanted in life can now be yours.

This will take some effort on your part, for in your endeavor to gain power and mastery over people, you will at times encounter strong resistance. Not all people will immediately do what you want them to do without questioning your methods. It will be up to you to find ways to deal with their resistance and overcome their objections so you can convert them to your way of thinking.

The real key to dealing with resistance and overcoming objections is to offer your listener certain concrete benefits that will let him fulfill his basic needs and desires. This chapter will show you exactly how to do that. When you use the techniques that I'll give you here...

YOU'LL GAIN THESE TERRIFIC BENEFITS

1. People will always do what you want them to do.
2. They'll follow your instructions implicitly and obey your

orders without question.

3. You'll be able to put your ideas and proposals across to others easily.

4. You'll get your own way every time.

5. You'll gain complete power and absolute mastery over others

TECHNIQUES YOU CAN USE TO GAIN THESE VALUABLE BENEFITS

Getting your message across to someone so he'll do what you want him to do depends as much upon his listening level as it does upon the words you use. If you use short simple words and avoid vague and abstract ones, you can be sure your listener will understand you. But that in itself is not enough. Your success will also depend upon his listening level.

Whenever you talk to someone, he'll be hearing you on only one of three wave lengths: *the nonhearing level; the semi-listening level; the thinking or comprehension level.*

1. *The Nonhearing Level.* At this level of comprehension, you're not even registering with your listener. He's not listening to you at all. His mind is concentrating only on what he wants to think about and what he himself is interested in.

A wife often finds that her husband uses this level to carry on a so-called conversation with her, especially in the evening after he's eaten and settled down in his easy chair in front of the TV.

If he's reading the paper, he might lower it once in a while to look at his wife, and even talk occasionally, saying things like, "Yes, dear, that's right...I see...then what did she say?" But he really isn't listening to her at all.

2. *The Semi-Listening Level.* At this level, your listener is remembering some of what you're saying. If you were to stop suddenly and ask him what you've been talking about, he'd no doubt be able to repeat your last sentence or so or at least tell you what your last idea was.

However, he really hasn't absorbed what you've been saying.

As soon as you stop talking, your ideas immediately disappear from his mind for he's not thinking seriously about them at all.

3. *The Thinking or Comprehension Level.* This is the level that you want your listener to reach so you can put your ideas across to him and get him to do what you want him to do.

How can you tell when his mind has reached the thinking level? When he asks you questions, voices objections, and offers resistance. So don't be upset or worried when he does this. This is exactly what you want to happen.

You see, when your listener presents a counterargument or voices an objection, this indicates he's interested in what you're saying. He wants to know more. If he were not interested, he wouldn't ask you anything. Your next step, then, after you have your listener at the thinking level, is to deal with his resistance and overcome his objections. Here's how to do that:

How to Overcome His Objections: Step One

In Chapter 1, I told you about the insurance salesman who researched hundreds of interviews to find out why people bought or failed to buy. He discovered that in more than sixty percent of cases, the first objection raised against buying insurance was not the real reason at all.

He found that a person almost always has two distinct reasons for doing anything: *a reason that sounds good to the listener,* and *one that he keeps hidden all to himself.*

You should always make sure you've found the hidden or real reason for your listener's resistance. To find the deep or hidden reason for a person's objections, simply keep asking one or all of the following three questions:

1. Why or why not?
2. And in addition to that?
3. Is there any other reason?

Be persistent about this. Eventually the real reason will surface. Usually you'll hear something along this line: "Well, to tell you the truth...," or "Well, if you really want to know why..." When you hear phrases like these, you'll know that the real objection is coming next. The moment you know the real reason for the person's resistance, you can take the next step to overcome it.

How to Overcome His Objections: Step Two

The best way to overcome your listener's objection is to turn it into a benefit. Let me show you how Charlie Rogers, a lubricating oils salesman, does this.

"One of the major objections a prospect usually voices is that although the product is good, the price is too high." Charlie says. "Now when your prospect offers this kind of objection, you can react in one of two ways.

"You can take the objection as an insurmountable obstacle or as a defeat, pack up your sample case, and leave.

"Or you can take that objection and turn it into a benefit to make a sale that otherwise could not be made. My answer to 'the price is too high' objection goes something like this:

"'Mr. Prospect, a cheap product costs you twice the price because you have complaints, mishaps, and you lose valuable customers. I'm offering you an excellent product at a fair price.

"'Into it go the highest quality materials and processes that give top-notch performance for your customer. The high-grade performance of my product is a result of years of experience and know-how in the oil business.

"'My company produces this lubricant at the least possible cost and sells it at the lowest possible price. If a less expensive method of production could be developed, my company would be the first to use it so the price could be lowered for you.'

"If the prospect still hesitates, I say, 'You must make the final decision, of course, but I hope you realize that *buying cheap to save money is like stopping a clock to save time!*'

"This last remark really makes my prospect stop and think. It results in a sale more often than not."

How successful is Charlie in converting objections into benefits so he can make sales? Well, he moves three times as much oil as any other salesman in his company and is in line for promotion to regional sales manager.

Now you may not be a salesman, but you can use this technique of changing an objection into a benefit in any sort of situation you can think of. For instance, does your wife object to going on a fishing or camping trip in the mountains for your annual vacation? You won't get anywhere arguing with her about it. All you'll do is increase her resistance. Figure out how to turn her objections into a benefit for her and you'll get your own way every time.

How to Overcome His Objections: Step Three

Logic, reason, and common sense are simply not enough to enable you to deal with a person's resistance, overcome his objections, and persuade him to see things your way. To completely overcome a person's objections so you can get your own way every time, you must appeal to his emotions.

Let me give you a specific example of how the emotions of the heart can completely overcome the reasoning and logic of the mind. Take love, for instance.

How many times does a girl marry the man her parents did not prefer? Mother had her eye on the young banker or doctor who had money, a promising career, social status, and a promising position in the community. Or maybe Dad had picked the brilliant young attorney who was headed for the governor's mansion.

But daughter married the milkman, the farmer, the shoe salesman, the rock musician, the garage mechanic, the grocery clerk. Why? Well, Mom and Dad picked their daughter's potential husband with their heads. Daughter picked him with her heart. The moral of this little story is quite simple:

People are ruled by emotions more than by logic and reason. This is not to say that daughter was wrong, even though in view of today's divorce rate, you might think so. I'm not saying that anyone's right or wrong. I'm only explaining why people do the things they do.

A person doesn't have to be in love to be emotionally involved. Check back on your own life and see how many of your own decisions—other than falling in love—were made on an emotional basis. If you didn't make most of your decisions that way, then you're a lot different from most of us.

Almost everything the rest of us do—buying cars, moving to a different house, changing jobs—is done on impulse, the way we *feel* about a certain thing at a particular moment of time, logic and reason be damned, no matter what the consequences.

So if you want to deal with a person's resistance and overcome his objections, then appeal to his emotions. Oh, you should appeal to his good judgment by all means. Always give people a logical and sensible reason for doing what you want them to do.

But if you really want to gain power and mastery over people; if you want to get action from them; if you want to get your own way every time; then appeal to one of their basic emotional drives. Just remember the next idea and you'll never go wrong:

The head never hears 'til the heart has listened.

A Specific Technique You Can Use to Deal with Your Listener's Resistance

You can use a specific kind of question to break down the barriers of your listener's resistance. This sort of question can be used to change a person's position, influence his way of thinking, or get him to make a firm commitment.

This technique is applicable to all sorts of situations. Suppose, for example, that you're trying to sell a product or service or idea or get a person to see things your way.

Somewhere along the line, whenever it seems most appropriate, you simply ask, in effect, "If I show you how and where you can benefit, will you buy my idea (or product or service or whatever)?"

Now your listener either has to say yes or he has to say why he doesn't want to go along with you. Either way you force his hand in the matter.

If he says *yes*, you're in good shape. If he says *no*, he still has to bring his objection out into the open where you can see it. You are now in a position to deal with his resistance and overcome his objection by changing it into a benefit.

This technique is so simple and easy to use that people tend to shy away from it at first, feeling it can't work. But it's an effective way to gain power and mastery over people so you can get what you want from them. Use it; you'll find it works like magic for you.

A Guaranteed Technique for Winning Every Argument

Almost every day, some circumstance will arise where you need to get another person to accept your viewpoint or see things your way. Whether you accomplish that or not depends on which of the following methods you use.

The first method—and the one most people use to try to win an argument—is force. If you use force in an attempt to overpower or intimidate your opponent, your argument will turn into nothing more than a shouting match and an ego battle.

But this is a complete waste of time. You cannot win an argument by forcefully ramming your ideas down the other person's throat. The only way you can ever really win an argument is when you get the other person to change his mind.

To win an argument every time, you must work *with* human nature, not *against* it. If you want a person to see things your way, don't force your ideas on him. He must accept your ideas from within himself—*from inside his own mind*. Your ideas must become *his* ideas before he will accept them. When he has convinced himself that your viewpoint is correct, he will change his mind voluntarily. When he sees things your way, when he makes your viewpoint his viewpoint, you'll win your argument.

You can get a person to accept your ideas only when you appeal to his emotions as well as to his reason, logic, and common sense. As I've already said, *the head never hears 'til the heart has listened*. You cannot possibly win an argument until that happens. Here are six guidelines you can use to win every single time:

1. *How to Retain Control of the Argument at All Times.* Don't jump the gun and try to win by stating your side first. If you do, you'll reveal your position and expose your vulnerable points. When you try to get your licks in ahead of your opponent, you allow the initiative to pass to him. You want to retain control of the situation yourself.

Although it might sound paradoxical, the best way to do this is to let him state his side of the case first. Don't interrupt. Let him talk himself out so he'll exhaust himself.

It is an extremely good idea to get the person to repeat some of his key points or his sore spots. Letting him get it all off his chest helps him immeasurably. If you can get him to repeat his complaints several times, he literally drains himself emotionally. That makes it much easier for you to win.

2. *How to Probe and Explore His Argument.* Unless the person is ready to receive a particular idea, he is not likely to accept it. Lead him on an objective fact-finding survey of his position until you find a weakness in his argument.

When you find such a weakness, use it for your opening statement to persuade him to accept your point of view. When he sees that weakness himself, he'll become much more receptive to your ideas.

That's why you should always let him talk first. You get his ideas out into the open where you can probe them for weaknesses. The more he realizes there are some holes in his argument, the more willing he will be to accept your point of view.

3. *How to Know When to Take Action.* It's no use for you to take action until you know the person is receptive to change. Listen for comments like these: "I could be wrong on a point or two...I'm willing to listen to reason...I've never looked at it that way before...I could be mistaken on this one detail..."

When you hear expressions of self-doubt like these, it's a clear signal to you that it's time for you to take action and present your side of the case.

4. *How to State Your Side of the Argument.* The tendency is always to use the old forceful methods to win an argument. You must discipline yourself to avoid this bad habit of trying to show the other fellow up. Even if you out-talk him to the point where he can say nothing in rebuttal, *you still will not win until he accepts your viewpoint as his very own.*

It's a proven fact that the best way to state your case is to do so moderately, accurately, and with sincerity. Be enthusiastic, but don't let your enthusiasm carry you away emotionally so that you exaggerate or make too forceful an approach.

5. *Don't Be Greedy.* Most people who use force to argue try to prove the other person completely wrong on every single point. They insist on winning 100 percent. This is a mistake. A skillful

person, who uses persuasion rather than force, will always be willing to concede something to his opponent or give ground on some minor matter.

So be flexible. Compromise a bit; bend with the wind. Give in here and there on small points. Just follow this rule and you'll be safe: *Give ground on trifles; never on principles.* All you need is the wisdom to know the difference between the two.

6. *Help the Other Person Save Face.* Not being greedy or not insisting on winning your case 100 percent helps the other person save face. But you can do much more than that. Here's how:

Many times your opponent realizes that he's wrong. He's already changed his mind and wants to agree with you, but unfortunately his ego gets in the way. His pride prevents him from admitting his mistake. If you find your opponent in that spot, open the door for him. Help him find a way out of his dilemma.

One way you can do this is to suggest he might not have had all the facts when he made up his mind. You might say something like this: "John, if you didn't know about this, I can see why you made the decision you did. I'd have done the same thing."

Even if John did have all the facts, he'll grab at this lifeline you've just thrown him. All he needs do is say he didn't have that fact and he's out of his corner. You've achieved your goal. You've helped him save face.

When you help a person save face and keep from destroying his pride, you'll gain a friend who'll support you all the way. When that happens, you'll have gained complete power and absolute mastery over him.

11

How to Write Masterful Letters That Produce Results Every Time

Even in today's modern technical world, we still depend on the written word to communicate with each other. We use letters, interoffice memos, brief informal notes, all with the purpose of getting others to do what we want them to do.

What you say in your correspondence, and how you say it, are ever so important in your drive to gain mastery over people. Remember what I told you in Chapter 7: *When you can command words to serve your thoughts and feelings, you are well on your way to commanding people to do your will and serve your purposes.*

In this chapter, I want to show you how to write masterful letters so you can attain that goal of commanding people to do your will and serve your purposes.

How you write can bring you prestige, respect, influence, promotion and advancement. It can mark the difference between a low-paying menial job the rest of your life and advancement to an important executive position. How you write can give you great power over others, for it is as true today as it was hundreds of years ago that *men really do govern with words.*

MORE BENEFITS YOU'LL GAIN FROM MASTERFUL LETTERS

Besides the benefits of prestige, respect, influence, promotion, advancement, and power over people that I've just told you about, you can also gain these additional benefits:

1. *People will cooperate with you and do as you want them to do* when you write masterful letters that express your message with clarity and power.

2. *There'll be a genuine meeting of the minds* when you write masterful letters to gain clear communication and definite understanding.

3. *You'll achieve your purposes.* With powerfully written letters, goals can be reached, missions accomplished, objectives attained.

4. *You'll succeed in getting what you want from others,* for it's a proven fact that successful people know how to communicate their orders, commands, and requests to others.

5. *You'll definitely better your chances for getting ahead.* If you work for a big company, you'll improve your chances of getting ahead if you handle yourself well on paper. Learn to write clear and forceful letters, and you'll attract the attention of the brass upstairs where it really counts. Without a doubt, you'll be promoted long before the person who cannot express himself forcefully and clearly in writing.

TECHNIQUES YOU CAN USE TO WRITE MASTERFUL LETTERS

Six Basic Rules for Writing Masterful Letters

1. Know Exactly What It Is That You Want to Get Done

Many people fire off letters without having a clear idea of exactly what it is they want to accomplish. I'm sure you've been on the receiving end of letters like that. When you get through reading them, you wonder what it was the writer really wanted.

If you know your purpose in writing, if the objective you want to gain is clear in your mind, your letter can be clear and easy to understand. However, if your objective is vague and abstract, your writing will also be vague and abstract. Before you start any letter, know precisely *why* you are writing it. Figure out exactly what it is you want to gain.

Just as meaningful conversation should have a major purpose, so should your writing, whether it's a letter, an interoffice memorandum, whatever.

Writing, just like speaking, can normally be classified into three general categories:

1. *To order or command* someone to do something.
2. *To inform* someone of something.
3. *To persuade* someone to do something.

All three kinds of letters will be concerned with *who, what when, where, why, and how*, but the emphasis will be different in each case depending entirely upon the purpose.

For example, a *letter directing action* indicates *what* has to be done. An *informative letter* will usually tell a person *how* to do something. A *persuasive letter* is written to explain *why* a certain action should be taken by the reader.

Of course, these purposes can often overlap, as when you make a directive or a command more palatable or more acceptable by explaining the *how* and *why* as well as the *what*. If you were writing a persuasive memo to your boss asking him to approve the use of some new office procedure, you would emphasize *why* it should be used; that is to say, you would *stress the benefits to be gained*, but you would also explain *how* the new system would work.

So, even though you might have some minor overlapping in your letters, keeping these three basic categories in mind will help you find clear explanations or convincing reasons to back up the specific objectives you're after.

2. *Know Who Your Reader Is Going to Be*

Who is going to read your letter? A person with a college degree or one with an eighth grade education? You'll get your point across better when you use words and ideas that your reader can easily understand. Whether a person reads you loud and clear depends on *his* training, knowledge, and experience, *not on yours*.

If you're writing a letter to go on a bulletin board for all employees to read, you must write so clearly that the least educated person in the place can understand what you've said. I still remember the announcement I read on the company bulletin board when I was in the army during World War II. It said, "Men with complaints will be made in the orderly room today."

"A lot of directives here at the plant are written at college levels of readability and understanding," says Keith Moore, the office manager for a tire and rubber company. "The writer forgets that people of modest education must read them and act on them. I do my best to get everyone to keep their letters and memos simple enough for everyone to understand."

It is important for you to determine who your reader is going to be, too. Always ask yourself, "Who must read and understand this?" The answer should influence the words and ideas you use.

3. Lay the Proper Foundation

Masterful and powerful letter writing is based on proper preparation—the selection, analysis, and organization of your ideas. Your preparation may take only a few minutes, or perhaps several days. It depends on the size of your problem. Either way, it will be one of the most important parts of your writing efforts.

Many people write useless and ineffective letters because they start writing before they are actually ready to do so. That's why their letters aren't satisfactory and don't get the results they want.

So, before you pick up a pencil or sit down at your typewriter, think your problem through thoroughly before writing. First, get the answers to *who, what, when, where, why,* and *how*. Then, start on your actual job of writing.

4. Identify and Pinpoint Your Main Ideas

Successful writers of masterful and powerful letters know that deciding what to leave out is just as important as what to put in, if not more so. Words, ideas, and facts that are not essential to the understanding or the acceptance of your specific idea will only hide and weaken it.

It doesn't really matter whether your writing is based on your personal knowledge, on reading and research, or both. The problem you face is usually too much material rather than not enough.

Preparing to write is primarily a process of defining, sifting, and discarding until you have only one clear purpose or objective in mind left and the main ideas necessary to support it or reach it.

5. *Write from an Outline*

Any piece of writing, no matter what it is, can be done logically and quickly from an outline. If you're writing a long, several-page letter, you may need to work from a written outline. If it's a short letter, a simple outline in your head may be all that you need.

An outline makes your writing plan easy to see and helps you keep your specific objective clearly in mind. But it is worthless unless you stick to your outline and work from it. This is not to say you should not change your outline here and there if some better ideas occur to you. You should. Your outline should be a working sketch, not a final blueprint.

On the other hand, you should not let your writing get so far out of hand that it develops a case of elephantiasis. This can easily happen if you stray too far from your original outline.

6. *Review Your Writing for Objectivity*

Unless you're writing a chatty personal family letter or a love letter to your sweetheart, chances are you won't have a finished product ready to go on your first attempt. When you've completed your first draft, you should review and revise your work.

As you do this, concentrate on the objectivity of your writing. Business letters in particular should be objective, whether they're informative, persuasive, or directive in nature. When you present a decision or a recommendation to your boss, he will assume your letter is the result of careful thinking.

Staff studies and reports usually require you to discuss disadvantages and objections as fully as advantages, and from them to draw your measured conclusions and recommended courses of action. In letters and memorandums, however, you normally need to mention only briefly the disadvantages you have considered and set aside in favor of your recommended course of action.

How to Use "Power Words" That Get Your Reader to Take Action

By careful observation of people, you can learn which words are the most potent in creating a favorable reaction in others. But that takes time, so let me give you a head start.

For example, some words cause people to think rationally, using logic and reason. Other words cause them to react emotionally. Let me give you a specific example:

A real estate agent will tell the owner he'll be glad to sell his *house*. He doesn't use the word *home* when talking with the owner. Home is an emotional word and the seller can become reluctant to part with his home even though he's perfectly willing to get rid of his house. By the same token, the real estate agent never sells the buyer just a *house*. He always sells him a *home*.

These two words represent two entirely different ideas for the same object. A house is not a home, it's only a house. It is made of bricks, wood, and concrete. It's a very non-emotional idea. But a home is where your heart is, where your family lives, where your kids grow up. It is an extremely emotional word.

Emotional words are power words, and people are ruled by emotion more than by logic and reason. Salespeople always like to use emotional words because they cause people to buy. A top salesperson will never ask a prospect what he *thinks* about a product. Instead, he'll always ask him how he *feels* about it.

Think is a non-emotional word that requires a person to use logic and reason. But *feel* is an emotional word that goes straight to the heart, and remember, *the head never hears 'til the heart has listened*.

So, build up your own arsenal of emotional power words that are usable in your own particular situation, no matter what it is.

Another point well worth mentioning here about power words is this: You should learn which words turn your boss on and which ones turn him off, for no matter what they are, these are power words, too. Everyone has certain likes and dislikes when it comes to language, so you'd be smart to use the "pet" words your boss likes to hear. Remember that people generally like to hear their favorite words and phrases played back to them. Emulation of a person is still one of the highest forms of praise when subtly done.

How to Use the "Hook Technique" In Your Letters

To get your reader to take action and do what you want him to do, especially in the persuasive type of letter, you must use the "hook technique." No letter is complete without the hook. You may have written a wonderfully interesting and persuasive letter. It could be that you've aroused your reader's attention, captured his interest, and sparked his desire; but if you don't hook him, he will not take the action you want him to take.

Your reader will do what you want him to do for one of two reasons. The first is that you've made him so anxious to get what you've offered, he'll take the required action immediately. But most people tend to procrastinate. They want to think it over so they put things off for a while. You must give him another reason to take action. That's where the hook comes in.

You must make this kind of reader understand how he's going to lose out if he doesn't immediately do as you ask him to do. The hook provides a penalty if your reader fails to take action. That is the second reason the reader will do as you ask. Unless your hook arouses fear in your reader that he will lose something worth while if he doesn't act at once, you won't get the results you want.

Fear is on the opposite side of the coin of desire. If you can't move a person to action by arousing his desire, then turn the coin over and move him to action by arousing his fear.

For example, I have a letter in front of me right now from the savings and loan association that holds the mortgage on my home. Since my house was bought before interest rates skyrocketed, the bank is anxious for me to pay my loan off so they can lend that money out again at nearly twice the interest I'm paying.

In fact, they are so anxious for me to do that, they are offering me a discount of several thousand dollars on my present loan if I will pay it off or refinance it. Their letter says that my discount may be as high as twenty-five percent! That's a healthy saving for me and naturally I'm interested, for I'm as desirous of saving money as anyone else.

But to make sure that I will take action without delay, they closed their letter with the "hook" I've just described to you. Their hook says: "ACT NOW! This offer is for a limited time only and may be withdrawn without prior notice!"

Even the government tax people are smart enough to get into the act and use a hook to collect taxes quickly. My property tax bill offers me a four percent discount if I pay my taxes in the same month I receive my bill. If I do not, then I have to pay the full amount, and if I wait too long, I not only have to pay the full amount, but also a penalty.

Since the hook technique is usually used in a letter where you're persuading someone to do something, I want to give you an excellent format that you can use for just such a letter.

Format for a Persuasive Letter Using the Hook Technique

1. *The Opening.* Here you grab your reader's attention at once by fitting in with his train of thought (one or more of the fourteen basic needs and desires all people have). You establish your point of contact with your reader's self-interests to excite and arouse his curiosity so he will read further into your letter.

2. *You Cover the Benefits to Be Gained.* As soon as you have your reader's attention, tell him how he's going to benefit by doing as you ask. Give him a reason or motive to take action. Do this, not merely by describing what your product or your proposal is, but by *letting him know what it will do for him.* Tell him about the profit, pleasure, convenience, and so on, that he will gain.

3. *Offer Proof of What You Say.* The best proof you can offer that your proposition will give him the benefits you've indicated is to tell him of others who've benefited, too. Let him check with Sam Jones, Sally Brown, or Joe Gray so he can find out for himself that you're telling him the truth.

If you're going to bring on your witnesses, you must use actual people who are willing to let you use their names, addresses, phone numbers, etc. This requires some extra effort on your part, but there is absolutely no better way to gain a person's confidence and trust in you and in what you say.

4. *Tell Him How He Can Gain Those Benefits.* This is usually done in the next to last paragraph of your letter. Here you give your reader his exact instructions. You tell him exactly what he must do to gain the benefits you've offered him.

5. *Close with the Hook.* This is the snapper or the penalty that you hold over your reluctant reader's head. You hook him and force him to take action by telling him about the loss in money or prestige or opportunity that he will incur if he does not act at once. You normally place the hook in the last paragraph of your letter.

A time penalty is one of the best ways to get the action you want. For example: This offer expires in five days...Good only until the 15th of March...Prices go up next month...Limited supply: first come, first served...Act now! This offer is for a limited time only and may be withdrawn without prior notice...Four percent discount good only through the month of November.... The last two are the ones specifically used by my savings and loan association and the county tax collector.

Now, on to the next chapter where we'll discuss a subject that has been of interest to all mankind since the days when Adam and Eve first walked in the Garden of Eden: "How to master and control the opposite sex."

12

How to Master and Control the Opposite Sex

Mastering and controlling the opposite sex does not mean that a secretary has to come across or else, although that's the first interpretation some might assume from this chapter title. Nor does it mean that the sweet young thing on the production line has to go to bed with her supervisor to keep her job. Mastering and controlling the opposite sex has nothing at all to do with this kind of behavior, at least in my mind.

Several situations having to do with men and women working together come to mind that can be more profitably discussed when talking about how to master and control the opposite sex. For example, how can the female executive master and control the opposite sex so she can succeed in a man's world? Or how can she develop the mystique of power she'll need so much? I'll cover these two examples and others in this highly informative chapter.

Of course, I'm not opposed to a romantic view of mastering and controlling the opposite sex in the appropriate situation, so I also want to show you how to get your own way with your mate, be that mate a husband or wife, boyfriend or girlfriend.

If you're having trouble with your marriage, or if you're having other romantic problems, you can forget them when you use the extremely simple but highly effective technique I'll tell you about toward the end of this chapter.

Perhaps you feel you've been cheated out of a truly great romance, that love has passed you by. I can assure you that it's not too late, no matter how old you are. You can use this same technique to create a brand-new you, a new lover who can attract anyone he or she wants to.

BENEFITS YOU'LL GAIN BY MASTERING AND CONTROLLING THE OPPOSITE SEX

1. When you master and control not only your own sex, but also people of the opposite sex in your work or business, *you'll become a true master of others in the art of dealing with people.*

2. When you show your boss that you're an expert in handling the opposite sex, *you'll be earmarked for greater things.* If you're a man, this is highly important, for most men—even the most powerful ones—feel completely helpless when dealing with a woman. If you're a woman, you can take advantage of this male weakness.

3. When you control and master the opposite sex, *you'll gain immense power with people.* I'll give you several highly useful techniques you can use to develop this mystique of power.

4. On the romantic side, when you know how to master and control your husband or wife, your boyfriend or girlfriend, *you will be able to get your own way every time.* To help you gain that goal, I'll reveal a hidden secret that will literally work miracles for you.

TECHNIQUES YOU CAN USE TO MASTER AND CONTROL THE OPPOSITE SEX

How to Be a Successful Woman in a Man's World

Whether women like it or not, the business world is male territory. Right or wrong, men still call the shots. A woman entering this world for the first time may suddenly feel as if she's knee-deep in quicksand. Sure, women have made big gains in the business world, and a lot of them have developed extremely successful careers. But when it comes to complete equality, women still have a long way to go.

However, if you know what you want and are willing to follow the methods I'll give you here, you can succeed. No one can stop you if you have enough determination. I want to give you five techniques that will help you develop a successful career as a woman. I know there are others, but I feel that these five are the most important, especially in the beginning.

1. *Know Exactly What Your Goal Is.* The first step in becoming a successful woman in a man's world is to know exactly what your goal is. This might sound ridiculously simple to you, yet I have talked to scores of young businesswomen in my Seminars for Female Executives who say they want to accomplish great things in business, but they don't have the slightest idea what those great things are: They've set no goals for themselves, they say, because they aren't sure how high they can go as women in a man's business world.

My answer to this is that you can go as high as your capabilities will take you, whether you're a woman or not. If you can do the job, don't limit yourself by creating obstacles and barriers that don't exist except in your own mind.

Determine exactly what specific goal you want to attain. Do you want to be chairman of the board or president of your own company some day? Is this your dream? Then dedicate yourself toward achieving that goal with unswerving singleness of purpose.

2. *Give It Your Best Shot.* Once you know what you want, go after it with everything you've got. Use every means available to you. Going after what you want requires persistence and plain dogged determination, not giving up, not quitting at the first setback. If you've developed your mental and intellectual resources and are ready for the long haul ahead, you'll have sufficient strength to follow-up and insure your continued success.

The female president of a Chicago executive placement firm told me this: "Men in management are afraid that even the most enthusiastic woman executive will drop everything for the first appealing man who comes along. Marriage is the biggest single reason women scrap their career plans. When the going gets rough, marriage can look like an easy out."

There is no doubt about it; marriage can change things. A great many times the new wife will pay more attention to her husband and social activities than she does to her job and her career. But you can be successful at both if you keep your priorities in line.

3. *Learn to Get Along with Your Boss.* If you want to get ahead and stay there, you have to get along with your boss. No one is more important to you and your career than the man or woman who can get you promoted or raise your pay.

You'll always get along better with your boss if you're known as a hard worker. Nothing makes a boss happier than the sight of an employee toiling away at the job. Looking busy, sounding busy, and being busy are not only smart office politics, but also simply good business, period.

However, being a good worker is not enough. Another important way of getting along with your boss is to reinforce and build up his self-image while doing the best job you can for him. Make your style mesh with his. If he works at a rapid-fire pace, give him fast and concise answers—bare facts stated briefly without embellishment. If he enjoys hearing a lot of detail, give him that. Always follow his lead. After all, he's the boss.

4. *How to Rebuff His Advances Without Destroying Him or Yourself.* If your boss makes a serious pass at you, you want to turn him off without destroying both his ego and yourself. Don't be like the young female executive who said, "To hell with his ego and his feelings! He's the one who made the pass, not me!" She then proceeded to ridicule him to every woman in the company. You can guess how long she lasted.

The best way to let your boss down easily is simply to say, "I'm sorry, but I'm already committed; there's somebody else I care for very much." This allows him to withdraw gracefully without hurt pride or anger for you haven't rejected him for himself.

If this should fail, tell him that your husband or boyfriend is insanely, even murderously, jealous. It's amazing to see how quickly a man will lose interest in an office romance when he finds out the results could be dangerous to himself.

5. *Learn to Delegate Responsibility.* This is the most distinguishing hallmark of the successful executive. Unfortunately, a common mistake that many female executives make is in not delegating responsibility properly. Watch the men around you. See how the competent ones do it. Smart male executives will chop up an assignment—no matter how small it already is—and pass various tasks around to their subordinates to do. Even when it might be quicker to do the job themselves, they will not do so.

Women, on the other hand, tend to hang onto every detail of an assignment, even when it's large and complex. They are afraid that if something goes wrong, they'll get all the blame. If you do this, you'll limit your effectiveness. You'll be passed over for promotion, for it'll be obvious to your superiors that you can't handle anything bigger or higher than what you are handling right now.

So don't hesitate, delegate. Every time you give something to someone else to do, you free yourself to accept more responsibility. Top management is always happy to know there is a capable person around to take care of new developments. Be smart; let that person be you.

The three key words for delegating responsibility are "organize," "deputize," "supervise." First, *organize the work to be done* by breaking it up into smaller pieces. Then, *deputize by passing out those pieces to specific people to do*. Finally, *supervise each individual's work* to make sure that it's being done properly and on time. There's no limit to what you can get done if you use this simple technique to delegate responsibility to others.

How a Woman Can Develop the Mystique of Power

My first recommendation is that you not use male power symbols. Develop your own. Let me give you some techniques to help you get started.

1. *Develop Your Own Self-Power Attitude.* Self-power must be real. It can't be faked. You must feel it inside you generating so strongly that other people will sense it, too. Your self-power must be so forceful that others will not even dare to criticize you. You need fear no challenge, for you are not inferior to anyone. You are the best.

2. *Hire a Male Secretary.* As an executive, you'll be entitled to a secretary, but don't hire a woman. Hire a man instead. This will increase your visible power tremendously. I know of nothing more intimidating than to hear a male secretary's voice on the phone saying, "I'm sorry, but Mrs. Brown is busy right now. Would you care to call back?"

Never let your secretary say, "May she call you back?" Make sure he always says, "Would you care to call back?" This establishes you as the dominant personality in this power duel. You are clearly the one in control.

3. *Where to Sit in a Staff Conference.* The second power

position is always to the left of the boss. This is true in both civilian and military circles. There is usually a straight-backed chair at this position. The number two person always sits there. Other seats are normally easy chairs and a sofa.

Get to the meeting first and sit down in this power seat. If anyone questions your right to do so, say that you have a back problem and your doctor insists that you not slump or sit in a soft chair. Chances are that no one will say a word, for after all, you are a woman, and no one expects you to know men's rules. Not only that, it would be rude to ask you to move.

You'll soon be regarded as a person of power on the way up, second only to the boss. Many a successful career has been properly kicked off simply by sitting in the right chair.

4. *How to Handle Male Visitors to Your Office.* Chairs for visitors in your own office should be easy chairs or a sofa. When you are sitting in the power position behind your desk, and your male visitor is slumped down or sprawled out in an easy chair or sofa, he is immediately at a disadvantage. It's much easier for you to retain the upper hand psychologically when he's sitting in a weaker position.

5. *How to Challenge Someone Else's Power Play.* Did you ever stub your toe on a rock and then hurt your foot even worse when you kicked it? The rock is completely silent. It can't talk and tell you how it happened. No matter how much you yell or kick or cuss, it won't talk back. And the quieter it is, the madder you become.

You can use the rock's tactics on your challenger. Simply ignore him. Say nothing. Pay no attention to his commands, his threats, his blustering. The quieter you remain, the more flustered he will become. Hold your ground; he'll finally give up and leave you alone.

6. *How to Use the "Steepling" Technique.* Powerful people often make a "steeple" with their hands. Watch a group of people during a meeting. As the leader listens to a subordinate's suggestions, he will steeple. This shows that he is seriously thinking about what the other person is saying. As his thoughts become more profound, he may steeple in a higher and higher position until the steeple almost hides his face.

Medical doctors, psychiatrists, and psychologists are avid steeplers. The implication is they are deep thinkers and extremely intelligent people. Use the steepling technique and people will draw the same conclusions about you. This technique is a powerful adjunct you can use to turn off another person's play for power.

7. *Build Yourself Some Powerful Alliances.* Nobody "has it made" in the business world. Somebody dies, retires, embezzles some funds, becomes an alcoholic, suffers burnout from overwork, or cracks up with personal problems. Any of these things can send shock waves through the entire company, changing the power structure completely. Build some alliances for yourself so you can move in whatever direction the situation dictates.

How to Master and Control the Opposite Sex: For Men Only

You might think I've devoted too much of this chapter to women, but look at it this way: Those sections on "How to Be a Successful Woman in a Man's World" and "How a Woman Can Develop the Mystique of Power" can be useful to you, too, and here's why: When you know the "enemy's" tactics, you can be prepared to foil her plans and mount a counteroffensive of your own.

When you know your female competitor's plans, you will truly be in an enviable position, for you'll have unlimited power over her. Your best bet is to make up a dossier that lists her strong points and her most vulnerable ones. Then you can be prepared to attack. Never attack a strong point. Always go for a weak one where she cannot protect herself.

How to Master and Control Your Spouse (or Friend) and Keep Him (Her) Happy All at the Same Time

If you will recall, I told you in Chapter 1 how Barbara T's shaky marriage was saved when she learned to pay attention to her husband's basic needs and desires. You can use these same methods to master and control your mate and keep him happy all at the same time. Of the fourteen basic needs and desires that we all have, I've found that the desire to be important is the most dominant one of all in everyone. So, make your mate a VIP and you'll win every time; you'll never fail. Incidentally, I've used *him* in the following examples. If you're a man, simply replace the word *him* with *her*.

Make Your Spouse the Most Important Person in Your Life.
When you do that, you'll master him and gain complete control.
Let me give you three methods you can use to make this valuable
technique work:

1. *Think That Your Mate Is the Most Important Person in the
Whole Wide World.* The first rule is simply to convince yourself that
your mate is the most important person in your life. Do this, and
you won't have to pretend. Your own attitude will get across to him
even when you're not trying.

Not only that, you won't have to use gimmicks and tricks to
make this technique work. Your relations with your mate will be an
honest and sincere basis. As you think, so shall you believe, and as
you believe, so shall it be. Act as if it were true, and it will be true.

2. *Pay Close Attention to Everything He Says and Does.* The
most common complaint of wives and husbands is this: "He never
notices me...never pays attention to me...takes me for granted
...treats me like an old shoe."

Does your wife have a new hairdo? Tell her how beautiful it
makes her look. Is she wearing a new dress? Compliment her on her
choice. Thank her for the wonderful dinner. The same advice goes
for the wife, too. I once heard of a wife who was so tired of not
receiving any attention from her husband that she met him at the
door wearing nothing but a tiny kitchen apron when he came home
from work! You can bet he paid close attention to her from then on.

You may not need to go that far, but remember: if you want to
master and control him, if you want him to do as you desire, then
make him the most important person in the world. You can do that
by giving your rapt attention to whatever he says and does.

3. *Always Praise; Never Criticize.* Praise is the most powerful
technique you can use to feed a person's ego and make him feel
important. By the same token, criticism destroys. Criticism destroys people. It creates enemies. It destroys love and marriages. It
ruins friendships. In fact, I can think of nothing criticism does that
is of any value whatever to anyone.

If you want to master and control your mate, *never criticize
him.* Praise him instead. Praise creates energy. It makes a person
work harder, more efficiently, and with greater enthusiasm,

because praise makes the person feel proud of himself and what he has done.

Just say to your mate, "I am so proud of you." He'll do whatever you want him to do when he hears that. You just can't miss when you praise him for what he's done.

13

How to Turn Your Enemies into Devoted Friends

In this chapter, you'll discover how to counter the most treacherous people of all—those who use talk as a weapon trying to destroy you, glib people with slippery tongues who use malicious gossip and slander to discredit your reputation and credibility. But I'll show you not only how to stop them dead in their tracks, but also how to turn them into devoted friends.

A successful businessman and close friend of mine, Len W., once told me, "In business, even a single enemy is one too many. But you need not be afraid of those who are outspoken and leave no room for doubt that they are your enemies. You can cope with those people because you know exactly where you stand with them. It is the hidden enemy, the two-faced hypocrite, the one who speaks with the forked tongue, who will cause all your problems."

The first thing you need to do, then, is to *determine exactly who that hidden enemy is*. The second thing is to *destroy him so he will no longer be a threat to you*. Let me discuss each one of these points now in more detail.

1. *Know Who Your Enemy Is*. An enemy is not someone who will try to destroy you by brute force. No, your enemy will be much more subtle and crafty than that. He'll smile to your face and destroy your good name and reputation behind your back with gossip and slander. Let me give you a good example of that:

"Did you hear about Evans?" the rumormonger will ask in a whisper as if imparting a deep dark secret. "I heard it this morning in the cafeteria. He must be in hot water with someone upstairs.

Somebody saw him going into an employment agency the other day looking for a new job. Have you heard about that?''

No, of course, the other person hadn't heard about it because the rumor is entirely false. No one saw Evans at an employment agency because he'd never been to one. He wasn't in any trouble topside. But he soon will be when the false rumor gets around the office.

His loyalty to the company will now be questioned. When Evans hears the rumor himself, he will naturally deny it, but after all, that's what people would expect him to do. His denial unfortunately lends credibility to the rumor. And that rumor has killed his scheduled promotion. Guess who gets promoted instead!

So, always protect yourself at all times. Shore up your own defenses. Sit with your back to the wall. Or better yet, go on the attack yourself. The best defense is always the offense for then the other person must defend himself.

2. *How to Destroy Your Enemy.* Much as you might like to tear into the other fellow, take it from me, it won't work. You'll never destroy your enemy by fighting back. As long as you do battle with him, he'll be your enemy and do battle with you. What to do then?

Well, an old, old cliché says the only way to destroy your enemy is to make him your friend. Old or not, cliché or not, I can think of no better way to get rid of your enemy. Now I can hear you say, "It won't work all the time." I couldn't agree more, for I know there'll be exceptions. There always are. You might not win 'em all, but you'll gain the victory ninety-five percent of the time.

As a good general rule to follow, never let the person drag you down to his level. That can happen easily if you allow yourself to be drawn into a fight. But don't let someone else's inferiority overcome your superiority. Keep your own values in line.

I know it's hard not to hit the other guy below the belt when you're gasping for air just after he's belted you one right in the breadbasket, but instead of fighting back with his weapons of slander and gossip, kill your enemy with kindness. Treat him with courtesy and respect. You'll confuse him so much that he'll be at a loss as to what to do.

I do not mean to imply that you should turn the other cheek and let him hit you again; not by any stretch of the imagination.

Just don't retaliate in kind. Treat your enemy with civility and kindness, but protect yourself at the same time.

When you convert your enemies into friends, you can put down your gun and pick up your fishing pole instead. To tell you the truth, though, I doubt if it will ever happen. By that I mean enemies are just like weeds. As soon as you get rid of one, another one will pop up. So turning enemies into friends can become a full-time job. But all your efforts will be well worth while, for when you convert your enemies into friends...

YOU'LL GAIN THESE BIG BENEFITS

1. *You'll gain many, many true friends,* for if you're like most of us, you'll start out with lots of enemies to convert.

2. Converting an enemy into a friend shows *you have the ability to master and control others,* and that's a talent well worth developing to the fullest.

3. *People will learn to admire and respect you* when you gain their friendship. They'll do what you ask them to do, willingly and gladly. You'll have power with people that works like magic.

4. *You'll establish your reputation as an expert in the art of human relations,* for converting enemies into friends requires tact, diplomacy, and a skill that few people possess.

TECHNIQUES YOU CAN USE TO GAIN THESE BENEFITS

How Enemies Are Made in the First Place: Techniques to Avoid

I want to tell you about a few procedures that are guaranteed to create enemies for you. Avoid them at all costs. You'll be far ahead of the game when you do.

1. *Malicious Gossip and Slander Create Enemies.* An old adage goes like this: "If you can say nothing good about someone, then say nothing." I have never been able to understand why some

people take such a perverse delight in slandering another person. The only conclusion I've ever been able to reach is that when a person is in some sort of trouble, other people are so happy it didn't happen to them that they can't help talking about it. Unfortunately, they magnify and amplify it until the facts are so distorted that the end result is slander and malicious gossip. Let me tell you about something that happened to a friend of mine.

"Some years ago our youngest son was visiting us and became very sick," Norman told me. "He was so sick, he was carried into the hospital's emergency room in a near coma. He was severely dehydrated and barely conscious. For three days he lay in intensive care. Finally, after fifteen days of lab analysis, consultations, and so on, a final diagnosis was made. He had a severe case of diabetes.

"Now at the time our son was wearing his hair down to his shoulders and although I didn't care for his long hair style, I had said nothing. After all, it was his hair, not mine.

"But a particularly vicious-tongued neighbor of ours, who regarded every young person with long hair as a hippie or a freak of some sort, spread the word throughout the neighborhood that our son was a dope addict and had been taken to the hospital suffering from an overdose of drugs! After she learned from my wife that the diagnosis was diabetes, she retraced her steps, warning everyone never to repeat what she had said.

"But one of my oldest and closest friends told me what had happened. 'Don't ever tell that woman anything in confidence, Norman,' he said to me. 'She just can't be trusted.'

"I never retaliated in any way, but needless to say, our friendship was reduced to that of a mere nodding acquaintance. I later learned that this couple had moved from three previous homes simply because they had destroyed the relationships with their neighbors by slanderous gossip. I wonder how long it will be before they are forced to move again?"

So don't gossip or maliciously slander another person. Not only will you lose all your friends, but you'll also pick up a lot of enemies.

2. *Criticizing Someone or Telling Him He Is Wrong Is Another Sure Way of Creating an Enemy.* Last year, I was on the Chamber of Commerce committee that was responsible for soliciting money from businessmen to make up food baskets for the poor at Christmas time.

Gene Baxter and I went together on most occasions, feeling that it was easier to collect with two people instead of only one. One old grumpy fellow complained loudly about giving. "I don't believe in charity," he said. "Nobody ever gave me anything. The Bible says 'God helps those who help themselves!'

"I agree with you," I said, "but we're not asking for much. Besides, it's the children we want to help out. After all, they're not old enough to help themselves yet as you suggest."

After we left with his check in hand, Gene said, "Jim, I've never heard of that Bible quotation, have you?"

"No, Gene, I haven't," I said, "because it doesn't come from the Bible. But if we'd told him he was wrong, we wouldn't have his check, would we?"

There's no point in telling a person he's wrong. When you do, you're criticizing him and criticism destroys friendships. Not only that, it creates enemies. Most of us can't even stand being told that our watch is wrong.

If you're a boss or if you're planning on becoming one some day, I know there'll be times when you need to correct another person's mistakes. But that is far beyond the scope of this chapter or this book. I would suggest that you get a copy of my book, *Guide to Managing People**, and read the 8th Secret, "How to Say It with Flowers," where this subject is covered in complete detail.

3. *Ridicule Someone and He'll Be Your Enemy for Life.* When you ridicule someone, you deflate his ego and destroy his feeling of pride and importance. Ridicule maims and cripples people psychologically.

You see, a person will tolerate almost any insult, defeat, or injury, and accept it with some semblance of good grace. You can steal his wife, his job, his money, and although he won't like you for that, he'll probably tolerate it all up to a point and still treat you like a civilized human being.

But if you make fun of a person, if you belittle and ridicule him, or if you make a fool of him—especially in front of others— you'll have made an enemy for the rest of your life. Not only have you deflated his ego and injured his pride, but you've also

---

*James K. Van Fleet, *Guide to Managing People* (West Nyack, New York, Parker Publishing Company, Inc., 1968).

completely devastated his sense of self-respect, dignity, and self-esteem.

So, if you do ridicule someone and make fun of him, better load your shotgun, bolt the doors, and bar the windows, for he'll come after you—and that's for sure. The basic desire for revenge, vengeance, an eye for an eye, and a tooth for a tooth, can be a greater driving force than even the desire for importance or the desire for sex.

How You Can Make the First Move

If you want to make a friend out of an enemy, it's up to you to make the first move. Otherwise, nothing's ever going to get done. Let me give you an example of how you can take that first important step.

Once upon a time, there lived in the small town of Suburbia two neighbors named George and Jim. But they really were not good neighbors at all. They were at odds with each other, although neither of them could remember exactly why. They just knew they didn't like each other and that was reason enough.

So they lived in a constant state of bitter verbal warfare. Most of the time they would not even speak at all, although in the summertime their lawnmowers often rubbed wheels as they moved along their backyard battle lines.

Then, late one summer, George and his wife went on a two-week vacation. At first, Jim and his wife did not even notice they were gone. After all, why should they? They seldom spoke to each other, anyway, unless one of them had a specific complaint to register.

But, one evening just after he'd finished mowing his yard, Jim noticed how high George's grass was. It was especially obvious now that he'd just mowed his own.

It would also be obvious to anyone driving by that George and his wife were not at home and had not been there for quite some time, Jim thought. In fact, it was an open invitation for a burglar to break in, Jim mused. And then like lightning, a sudden flash of inspiration hit him. *Don't try to love your neighbor—just help him.*

"I looked at that high grass again and my mind rebelled just at the thought of helping someone I so thoroughly disliked," Jim says. "But in spite of all my efforts to blot the idea from my mind, it persisted. It just wouldn't go away. So the next morning I mowed his blasted lawn!

"A few days later, George and Dora came home on a Sunday afternoon. Shortly after they got back, I saw him walking up and down the street. He was stopping at every house in the block.

"At last he knocked on my door. When I opened it, he just stood there staring at me, an odd and puzzled expression wrinkling up his face.

"After what seemed like an eternity, he spoke. 'Jim, did you mow my lawn?' he finally asked. It was the first time he'd called me by my first name in a good long while. 'I've asked everyone else on the block. No one else mowed it. Jack says you did it. Is that true, did you do it?' His tone was almost accusatory.

"'Yes, George, I did.' I said, almost belligerently, for I was waiting for him to blow his stack at me for mowing his grass.

"He hesitated for a moment, as if searching for the right thing to say. Finally he muttered in a low, almost inaudible voice, 'Thanks,' and then turned sharply and walked quickly away."

And so the ice had finally been broken for George and Jim. Oh, they're not playing golf or bowling together yet and their wives don't run back and forth every five minutes or so to borrow sugar or salt or chitchat. But they are making progress. At least they are smiling at each other as their lawnmowers pass. They even say "Hi!" once in a while. Their former backyard battleground is now a demilitarized zone. And who knows? They might even share a cup of coffee one of these days.

Turn an enemy into a friend with love? Perhaps, but only if you spell the word *love* H-E-L-P! How can I be so sure of that? That's easy—I'm Jim!

The Wrong Office Politics Makes Enemies; the Right Office Politics Makes Friends

Politicians aren't the only people who practice politics. Just what is politics anyway? Well, in the business world politics simply means getting along with people—your boss, your associates, your subordinates, your customers—and getting things done.

One of the quickest ways to make enemies is to seek personal gain at someone else's expense. Let me give you an example of how this kind of office politics can backfire.

Take the case of Earl. His boss, Allen, was away on summer vacation, and Earl was placed in temporary charge of the department. Allen's boss called for some information that Allen had been asked to get for him. Earl thought that this would be an excellent opportunity to impress Allen's boss and show him how undependable Allen actually was.

"Allen was hoping you wouldn't ask for this information until he got back from vacation, so he put off doing it," Earl told the big boss. "But I'll be glad to get it for you. I'll have a report into you this afternoon."

In one stroke, Earl thought he had lowered Allen's standing and raised his own prestige in the eyes of the big boss. When Allen came back, his superior called him in and told him about the incident. "I think we'd better keep an eye on Earl," he said. "I don't believe he can be trusted. It could well be he's already reached his top. In fact, we might even have to let him go."

If Earl had used the right office politics, he wouldn't have created this problem for himself. All he needed to say when Allen's boss called for the information was something like this:

"Allen was gathering up this information for you just before he left on vacation. He was so swamped with last-minute work, he gave me the job to do. He said to be sure to have the report ready for you when you called for it. I'll make a few last-minute changes and get it up to you this afternoon. All the material is assembled, waiting to be typed."

This approach would have made Earl a real comer in the eyes of Allen's boss. It would have shown that he was reliable and efficient, and a person who could be depended on to get the job done.

Sometimes it's necessary for you to master a person the moment you meet him. In the next chapter you'll learn an amazing strategy that lets you put complete strangers under your control immediately.

14

An Amazing Strategy That Lets You Master Total Strangers Immediately

Do you feel at a loss about what to do or what to say when you meet a stranger? Do you want to hold the upper hand, but don't know how or where to begin? Perhaps you'd like to gain power over others, to master and control them the first time you meet, but you don't really know how to do so. Maybe you'd just like to get better service from a waitress or a clerk in a store.

In this chapter, I'm going to give you some techniques that will let you do all these things, and more. I'll show you how to get off on the right foot with strangers so you can master and control their attitudes and actions from the very beginning. When you know how to do that...

YOU'LL GAIN THESE EXTREMELY IMPORTANT BENEFITS

1. When you use the first technique I'll give you, *you will be able to assume control of the other person immediately*. You will automatically become the master in any situation.

2. Use the second technique, and *you'll be able to get deferential service* from a waitress, a store clerk, even a snobbish government bureaucrat.

3. The third technique will show you *how to get a complete stranger to go out of his way to help you*.

4. When you use the fourth technique, *you'll be able to strike up a friendship with a total stranger*.

5. Use the fifth technique, and *you can control the attitudes and emotions of complete strangers*. When you control their attitudes and emotions, you will as a simple matter of course be able to control their actions and reactions.

6. And finally, in the last technique, you'll learn how *you can retain complete control of the situation* when you are briefing some top-level executives or VIPs who are total strangers.

THE TECHNIQUES YOU CAN USE TO GAIN THESE BENEFITS

How to Assume Control of the Other Person Immediately

When two people meet for the first time, one will automatically become the leader and assume control of the conversation or the situation. The other person will then become the follower. You can always take control if you will simply remember that *everybody in the world is waiting for someone to tell him what to do*. So, let that someone be you. You'll find that this amazing strategy will put total strangers under your control instantly.

All you need do is take the initiative and you will immediately have the momentum on your side. If you adopt a positive attitude and assume that the other person is going to do what you want him to do, you'll find that ninety-five percent of the time he'll carry out your request or your command without hesitation or question. In five percent of cases, all he needs is a little extra push.

Other people will always accept you at your own appraisal of yourself. You are more responsible for how people accept you than anyone else. A lot of people worry about what other persons think of them. You can rid yourself of that fear if you will simply remember that *you are not responsible for what other people think of you. You are responsible only for what you think of yourself.* People form their opinions of you based upon the opinion you have of yourself.

If you act like a nobody and put yourself down, people will treat you like a nobody and put you down, too. But if you act like a somebody with authority, people will treat you that way. It is a truism that a person can have whatever allowances or liberties he takes without opposition. Take the place and attitude of a leader, seize control, and others will immediately acquiesce to you.

How to Get Superior Service from a Waitress, a Clerk, Even a Government Official You've Never Met Before

One of the deepest desires we all have is the need to be important; the craving to be appreciated. Every time you deal with a stranger, you can fulfill that deep craving he has with a few words that won't cost you a single penny. Just pay the other person an unexpected compliment of some sort.

For example, whenever I go to a restaurant, I make it a point to compliment my waitress in some way. Just the other morning, the one who brought my water and menu seemed grouchy and out of sorts. I was determined to change her attitude at once.

"What a lovely fragrance you're wearing," I said. "You certainly make an old man feel young and spry again!"

Her face brightened immediately and a smile appeared in place of the frown. "Thanks," she said. "That's the nicest thing I've heard all morning."

You can be sure my eggs were just the way I wanted them, over medium well, not too soft, not too hard, just right. There was extra jelly for my toast and my coffee cup was constantly filled without my asking, all because I'd paid her a simple compliment.

Did you ever want to get a table close up so you could see the show better in a nightclub? My wife and I were standing in a long line waiting for the dinner show in one of those fabulous Las Vegas clubs. The *maître de* was strolling up and down the long line looking at the guests. He was handsomely dressed in a dinner jacket and had a magnificent beard, the kind that only a few people like Hemingway, Kenny Rogers, or Kris Kristofferson can wear well.

"I wish I could grow a beard that looks as handsome as yours does," I said to him. "I've always wanted to grow one, but I've never had the courage. I've had to content myself with my salt and pepper mustache."

"Why are you standing back here in line when you have a reservation for a front table?" he asked with a sly wink. "Come up here where you should be and I'll see that you and your lady are seated immediately."

If you want to see the service improve next time you're in a restaurant or a busy department store, pay the waitress or the clerk an unexpected compliment and see for yourself how good things will start to happen for you right then and there.

How to Get a Complete Stranger to Go Out of His Way to Help You

If you want to control the attitudes and actions of a total stranger, if you want to get a person you've never met before to do whatever you ask him to do for you, then say something that will let the other person know at once that he is superior to you in some way.

The plain truth is that every person you meet feels he is better than you in one way or another. A sure way to his heart is for you to let him know that you recognize his superiority. All you need do is ask a person for his advice, his opinion, or his help, and he'll go out of his way to assist you.

I can well recall when I first became interested in bowling. Naturally, I didn't know how or where to begin. I was looking at bowling balls, shoes, wrist supports, and so on. The bowling alley manager was all tied up with the details of a league so he couldn't help me for the moment.

I lifted one ball after another off the rack by the counter only to put it back. Then I noticed a woman on my left smiling and watching me sympathetically.

"Can you help me out?" I asked, although I was hesitant to ask a woman, for some reason I am not able to adequately explain. "I've never bowled before and I don't know where to start."

"Sure, let me give you a hand," she said. "I'll be glad to show you the tricks of the trade and help you get started."

That lady spent the entire afternoon helping me select the right ball and shoes and teaching me the rudiments of bowling.

If you'll just be willing to admit that some person could be superior to you in some way, and then ask for help, you'll soon find that a tremendous number of benefits will come your way—even if you're a man and that superior being is a woman!

This technique is a natural for women to use, for men always love to help the "weaker" sex so they can show off their knowledge and superior power in front of them. So ladies, let them be chauvinistic when you can profit from it!

How to Strike Up a Friendship with a Total Stranger

It's ever so easy to strike up a conversation with a stranger if you get your mind off yourself and concentrate on what the other person is interested in. There are a variety of conversation openers you can use to control the situation and get the other person to talk, but the three I've found to be the most effective are, in the order of their importance, a person's name, his vocation, and his hobby. Let me show you what I mean:

1. *A Man's Name Is the Most Important Word in All the World to Him,* so all you need say is, "Your name fascinates me. I don't think I've ever heard it before. Would you tell me more about its origin and meaning?" Let me give you an example.

A friend of mine, Harry Bellows, is the district sales manager for a wholesale nursery house. His company had been trying for years to win a certain large retail account from a man named Peter Menosky. More than a half-dozen salesmen had called on this gentleman, but without results. Finally the president called Harry in and asked him to have a go at it.

"The first thing I did was to check with each salesman," Harry says. "Each one told me the same thing. Mr. Menosky was really touchy about how his name was pronounced and how it was spelled.

"So I went down to the library to find out the exact ethnic derivation of the name 'Menosky.' Then I went calling on him.

"As soon as I was ushered into his office, I said, 'I've been anxious to meet you for a long time, Mr. Menosky. You see, I've always been interested in the ethnic derivation of names. It's a sort of hobby of mine.

"'Now I know your name is Slovakian in origin, but I haven't been able to find out what it means. I know your first name, Peter, means reliable and dependable, but the library is unable to give me the meaning of your last name. Can you tell me?'

"Mr. Menosky glared at me and said, 'How do you know I'm

Slovak? How do you know I'm not Polish? All your salesmen seem to think so!'

"'Because your name is spelled with the suffix *sky*,' I said. 'If your name were Polish, it would be spelled with an *ski*.'

"'By golly, you're a smart fellow,' Mr. Menosky said. 'I think I'd like to do business with you!'

"He then told me about his father coming to the United States penniless and knowing no one. He talked for more than an hour about his family's origins, his father's native country, his own hobbies and interests. I left with the biggest order we'd ever gotten from a retail nursery. He's been our steady customer ever since."

I'm just as touchy as Mr. Menosky about my name. Mine is of Dutch origin. My grandfather came to this country from Rotterdam, Holland, in 1870. All my ancestors are Holland Dutch, not German, and I dislike being called a German just as much as Mr. Menosky disliked being called Polish. We may all be United States citizens, but we still have a feeling of ethnic pride about our names.

2. *Every Person Likes to Tell You What He Does for a Living.* All you need say is, "I've always been interested in your profession. Would you tell me something about your position and the work you do?" This is usually enough to keep the other person going for a good hour or more. In fact, you might end up feeling swamped with information, as I did when I asked a young computer programmer to explain his work to me. He told me so much about computers, I thought I was going to drown in technical terms. I felt about like my father did when he used to say that the preacher told him more than he wanted to know. But be patient. Remember your purpose is to master and control the other person for your own benefit.

3. *Ask a Person to Tell You About His Hobby.* Most people have an avocation of some sort, be it hunting, fishing, bowling, golf, gardening, music, whatever. In a great many cases, people are as expert in their avocations as they are in their professions, if not more so. And they always love to talk about their hobbies.

I have a neighbor I've mentioned before, a pharmacist by vocation, a botanist by avocation. Bill is a walking botanical encyclopedia and can give a person valuable free advice about plants, shrubs, trees, vines, and so on. He can look at a tree or shrub and tell you if it needs iron or magnesium, has too much water, not enough water, whatever. All you need do to become his A-Number-One friend is ask him something about his hobby.

How to Control the Attitudes and Emotions of Strangers

When you study physics or chemistry, you find that positive attracts negative, like goes with unlike, acid neutralizes alkali. But this doesn't hold true when you're learning how to master and control people. When you're dealing with human beings, just the opposite is true. Let me show you exactly what I mean:

- Be kind to others; they will be kind to you.
- Be mean to others; they will be mean to you.
- Be courteous to others; they will be courteous to you.
- Be rude to others; they will be rude to you.
- Be friendly to others; they will be friendly to you.
- Be hostile toward others; they will be hostile toward you.
- Smile at others; they will smile back at you.
- Frown at others; they will frown at you.

Just as I told you in the beginning of this chapter, whenever two people are involved in a relationship, one will be the leader, and the other will be the follower. If you assume the position of leadership as you should, the attitudes and emotions of others will depend entirely on your attitude and emotions. The power you have over others and your ability to master and control their emotions and actions is enormous.

In dealing with others, then, you will always see your own attitude reflected back in the other person's behavior. It is almost as if you were looking at yourself in a mirror. When you smile, the person in the mirror smiles. When you frown, the person in the mirror frowns back at you. Let me give you a simple example.

Take my grandson, Joel. When I smile at him, he's happy, and he smiles too. But if I frown the least little bit or if I act irritated and impatient about something, he gets a worried look on his face, and says, "Are you mad, grandpa?"

Then I'll smile back at him and reply, "No, of course I'm not mad. Are you?"

A look of relief and joy comes over his face, and he says, "Nope, I'm not mad either. I'm happy!"

You don't have to say a single word to influence another person. Smiles and frowns are both contagious. It's all up to you how you want to infect the other person. His attitudes and actions will depend entirely on your attitude and your actions.

How to Brief a Group of Top-Level Executives or VIPs Who Are Complete Strangers

First of all, if you're going to brief some top-level executives or visiting VIPs on your operation, remember, no matter what their status is, you are in charge. You are the authority. For those few moments of time, no matter how brief they are, you are the leader, and your audience, the followers. As I told you in the beginning of this chapter, other people will accept you at your own appraisal of yourself. This is the time to make that count.

Assume a positive attitude. Act as if it were impossible to fail and you'll find yourself capable of standing up before anyone—top-level executives, VIPs, the board of directors, city council, chamber of commerce, Kiwanis, you name it—and put them completely under your control.

You can become the leader of any group—neighborhood, religious, civic, fraternal, business, family, political—as long as you remember that *everybody in the world is waiting for someone to tell him what to do*. That's an amazing strategy that puts total strangers, and anyone else, for that matter, under your complete control instantly every single time.

In the next chapter I'll discuss a much tougher subject: "Getting Your Family to Do What You Want Them to Do." If you think getting strangers to do what you want is hard work, let me tell you this. It's a piece of cake when compared to your own family. After all, your family knows you. Strangers don't. That familiarity makes the job a lot tougher for you.

15

Getting Your Family to Do
What You Want Them to Do

The first question to ask yourself is what are you really trying to accomplish by controlling your family? If it is just to prove that you're the boss in your house, that's the wrong objective. That sort of attitude and action on a father's part will cause children to become rebellious and leave home as early as possible to get out from under the tyrant's iron hand. It can also quickly drive a wife to the divorce court. You cannot possibly get your family to do what you want them to do by using force or threats or by being a dictator.

But if you want to control your family so they will do what you want them to do *for their own benefit*, then you're on the right track. When the members of your family benefit by doing as you ask, so will you. Here are just some of the...

HUGE BENEFITS YOU WILL GAIN

1. Your family will look to you for guidance and direction.
2. They'll do what you want them to do without argument or question.
3. You'll be the lord and master of your house without any visible effort on your part.
4. There will be a peaceful, pleasant, and happy atmosphere in your home.
5. You'll gain love and respect from each member of your family.

6. A spirit of cheerful cooperation and helpfulness will be evident in your house.

7. There will be a willingness to work together to solve common family problems.

TECHNIQUES YOU CAN USE TO GAIN THESE BENEFITS

To Have Them Do What You Want, Use This Technique First

If you want to get, you first have to give. Don't expect to get something from your family and give nothing in return just because it's your family. If you want your spouse or your children to do something for you, then you must make the first move, and do something for them. Even in closely knit families that enjoy pleasant and harmonious relationships, the initial reaction to an order or a request is always "*What's in it for me*?" That's human nature and is to be expected. Perhaps that something you need to give them most of all is the *incentive* that will make them *want* to do as you desire.

I am reminded here of the fable of the old man who froze to death sitting in front of a stove with a huge pile of wood stacked up beside him because he was so stingy that he didn't want to use it.

"Give me some heat," the old man said, stretching out his frozen hands toward the cold stove. "Then I'll give you some wood to burn."

But it is impossible to give nothing and get something in return. That happens only in fairy tales. So don't make the mistake of thinking you can give nothing and get something back. By the same token, it's impossible to give something and get nothing in return.

A petty, shortsighted person often refuses to give because he cannot see how or where he's going to profit by so doing. He gets nothing back because he gives nothing away. So you see, the maxim holds true even in this case. Just like the old man who froze to death in front of a stove with a pile of wood stacked up beside him, he got nothing back because that's exactly what he gave away: nothing!

This fable of the old man is not at all farfetched. The same thing happens in real life. How many times have you picked up the paper to read where someone died in friendless "poverty" with thousands of dollars stored up in mattresses and cardboard boxes?

So remember that if you want your family to do what you want them to do, give them an incentive for doing it. Offer them a benefit when they do as you ask. Then you'll be sure they'll do as you desire. One of the biggest incentives you can use is to give them your love. When you do that, you'll get back love.

If you want to control your family and make them do what you want them to do, it's a prerequisite that you establish a cheerful and happy atmosphere in your home. If you are a kill-joy or have a critical attitude in your home, if you play favorites, or if you cause members of your family to feel constant fear and anxiety, you cannot possibly get the results you want. Don't expect your spouse or your children to do what you want if they are angry or filled with hatred or resentment toward you because of your dictatorial attitudes and actions. Let me show you now...

How to Create a Happy Family Atmosphere

Each and every one of us possesses a power we often fail to use properly. That power is the freedom of choice. Many people choose poverty when they need only to choose wealth. Some choose failure instead of success. Others choose to be afraid of life when all they need do is step out with courage and take what is rightfully theirs.

What you do about your family life is the same. You have the power to choose the kind of home life you want. You can choose one that is fun: one that is filled with excitement, joy, and happiness. Or you can choose a home life that is constantly filled with anger, resentment, arguments, and bickering. It's all up to you.

I had an uncle whom I admired a great deal, Warren Roland. Uncle Warren and Aunt Opal were married for more than fifty years when he died. They always were wonderfully happy with each other. I never once heard a harsh word from either of them toward the other, nor did I ever see an angry glance exchanged between them.

Just before I was married, Uncle Warren asked me to come by his place to chat. "Will you accept a small bit of advice from your old uncle?" he asked. When I said that I would be glad to, here's what he told me.

· "You can be happy in your marriage if you choose to be," he said. "That's what your Aunt Opal and I did when we were married many years ago. We chose to be happy. If you want your marriage to be successful, I recommend that you do the same: *Choose to be happy*. It's really just that simple if you don't complicate it.

"Sure, there'll be ups and downs. You won't be living on the mountaintop every day. No one can do that. You'll have some valleys in between that will be filled with sorrow, heartaches, and sadness. Your Aunt Opal and I have had those bad days, too. But we've weathered those storms because we made up our minds at the very start to be happy in our marriage no matter what happened.

"So if you choose to be happy in your marriage right here and now at the very beginning, and your wife does the same, then no matter what happens, your marriage will be a good one."

The worth of my uncle's advice has not been dimmed by the passage of time. As far as I'm concerned, it's still good so I'm passing it along to you. I've found it to be most valuable in our more than forty years of married life.

Even if you've been married a long time, it is never too late to make the choice to be happy with your wife or husband. No matter how bad things might seem to be at times, they'll always get better when you make that one simple decision. *Just choose to be happy*.

One small bit of advice about choosing happiness in your home is this: Always be pleasant to your family no matter how rotten you might feel inside: There's no point in making them miserable just because you're down in the dumps.

It is particularly important to develop the habit of pleasant and cheerful conversation when the family is all together. This is especially true at mealtimes. Do not upset everyone's digestion— including your own—by making the family meal a recitation of troubles, anxieties, fears, warnings, and accusations. Discipline and dinner don't go together. Make every meal a joyful and festive occasion.

A Technique That Will Work Magic in Your Marriage for You

One of the real secrets to complete joy and happiness in your home is *accepting your partner as he or she is*. Don't try to change your spouse and make him or her over into a second edition of yourself. Don't nag or criticize. You'll never change a person that way. Not only that, you cannot possibly control your family and make them do what you want by using criticism.

Take your own husband, for instance. Have you ever been able to change him very much through all your years of marriage by nagging and finding fault with him? I know you probably thought you had good intentions. You felt you could make him over into the person you thought he ought to be, but did you ever really succeed? I doubt it; I know my wife never did.

If you're thinking of making your wife over to fit your own specifications by using criticism, forget it. I failed at that one, too. I haven't been able to change her one bit through all these years. She's still the same woman I married. But I'm glad I failed in this. I realize now that I couldn't have improved on her at all.

This is a most valuable point for you to remember. *The only person you can ever really change in your life is you, yourself, and you alone—no one else.* So accept your partner just as he or she is. You'll be much happier when you do.

For instance, I once knew a woman whose husband had a real problem and she desperately wanted to change him. Mrs. K. had a family of five children and a husband who'd been drunk and out of work for nearly all of their twenty-five years of marriage. She had supported the family most of that time herself by working in a department store.

Every possible treatment and approach that had been tried to solve her husband's alcoholism had failed. None had afforded him any lasting relief. For specific religious reasons, Mrs. K. did not want to divorce her husband, but at the same time, she could not accept him the way he was. And since she was unable to change him, her misery and despair became deeper and deeper.

Then, one day she made the most important discovery of her married life. "There is absolutely nothing I can do to change Dan or solve his drinking problem for him," she told herself. "But that is his problem, not mine. I'm powerless to change him or to solve his problem for him. I cannot live his life for him. He is a sick man, an alcoholic, and I am going to give up the idea right now that I can ever get him to stop drinking. From now on, I am not going to torture myself with his problem. I am going to accept things exactly the way they are.

"I will take care of him, of course, for he is my husband, and I love him in spite of everything. But I am going to quit trying to change him. I am going to accept him just as he is and do whatever I can to make my own life and the lives of my children as happy as possible under these circumstances."

Mrs. K. was finally admitting to herself that she was powerless to change her husband. Her new concept of the situation worked wonders for both herself and her children. It did not stop her husband from drinking; only *he* could do that. But, in spite of his drinking problem, Mrs. K. and her children all began to live comparatively normal and happy lives again.

Realizing that you cannot possibly change your husband or your wife can help you the same way. In fact, you'll never be able to achieve total joy and happiness in your marriage until you do accept your spouse exactly as he or she is.

This doesn't mean you can't guide, direct, and control your family when you accept them as they are. You can still get them to do what you want them to do just as long as you offer them a concrete benefit for doing so. Just refer to your list of fourteen basic needs and desires and you can always come up with one or more that fills the bill for you.

Use This Technique: Your Family Will Always Do What You Want

To love and to be loved are basic needs of every human being. Some couples think those are the only requirements for a happy marriage. But there's much more to love than the physical fulfillment of sexual desire. For instance, praise from you for what your mate does is also a part of true love.

When you use praise instead of criticism, you are fulfilling a basic human need. If you criticize, you're falling right into that old rut of trying to make your spouse over to fit your own standards and, as you've already seen, that doesn't work. So always use praise instead of criticism to get results. It'll pay you rich dividends.

Do you have any idea how many of the fourteen basic needs and desires you can fulfill for your spouse when you use praise? Let me list them so you can see for yourself what a valuable tool praise can be for you.

1. Recognition of efforts, reassurances of worth
2. Approval and acceptance
3. A feeling of importance, ego gratification
4. The accomplishment or achievement of something worth while
5. A sense of personal power
6. Self-esteem, dignity, self-respect
7. Love
8. Emotional security

When you can fulfill eight of fourteen basic needs and desires by using praise, it makes good sense to use it. There is most definitely power in praise.

If you are the husband, you can praise your wife in any number of ways. For example, if your morning coffee is good, then tell her so. (If it isn't, tell her so anyway!) Be generous with your praise. Don't wait until she does something big or unusual to praise her about. Praise her for her excellent cooking, her magnificent housekeeping, her beautiful appearance, her marvelous new hair-do. And don't forget to say "Thanks!" The two simple words, "Thank you," can be a real morale booster to a tired and worn-out housewife.

How a Wife Can Help Her Husband Become Successful

A wife can help her husband become successful by the simple act of praising him for what he does. If you want your husband to get ahead and be successful in his work, then praise him. Praise builds his self-confidence. Let me show you what I mean:

Armand L., president of a huge corporation employing several thousand employees, told me that big businessmen and corporation executives want to find out something about a man's wife before they promote him to a top-level responsible position.

"We are more interested in whether she gives her husband a feeling of confidence in himself than we are in her good looks and social acceptability," Armand says.

"You see, if she accepts her husband, if she gives him the

feeling she is pleased with him, and if she praises him in every way possible, it's about like getting a shot in the arm every time he comes home. His wife's praise sends him off each morning filled with the self-confidence that he can lick any problem that comes his way. And that's the kind of person we need in our top executive slots."

Praise works just as well on children as it does on husbands and wives. Let me show you how you can use praise to get your children to do whatever you want them to do.

How to Guide, Direct, and Control Your Children Without Effort

To guide, direct, and control your children without effort so they will always do what you want them to do, *make them happy*. When they're happy, they'll be only too glad to do as you desire.

How do you make a child happy? It takes a lot more than money and material possessions. You can start by giving your child your full attention. This is something a child usually needs the most and gets the least of. As a result, children often feel left out. Lack of attention makes them unwanted. You can give them a real sense of being wanted and fulfill their deep need for emotional security by giving them your wholehearted attention.

And praise is the best way I know of to give a person your full attention. Children respond to praise just as adults do. If you want your son or daughter to get better grades in school, then praise them. If you criticize their grades, they'll go even lower. I guarantee it. I know that from personal experience. You see, mine has been a learning process, too.

I know that sometimes you must discipline your children. After all, I raised three of my own. Discipline should be reasonable and firm, yet pleasant. Parents in unhappy families don't realize this, but in a happy family there is seldom any reason for discipline.

So give your children a happy, pleasant atmosphere, play with them, work with them, make them feel they belong by letting them take part in family projects, and you'll find that most disciplinary problems disappear. They'll do what you want them to do. When discipline is handled in this way, you can enjoy your children, too, just as Mike Turner does.

"One summer a few years ago when Gary was sixteen, he and I

went on a month-long trip throughout the West in a camper; just the two of us," Mike told me. "We did everything together just as two buddies would. We took turns driving the pickup truck, cooking the meals, washing the dishes, and making the beds. Not once during that month did I tell him what to do. I treated him as an equal.

"When we were back home, Gary paid me a compliment I will always remember, 'Dad, this has been the best time of my life,' he said. 'I'll always remember this trip, for I've learned that you're my friend as well as my father.'"

I know you must give guidance and counsel to your children, but if you really want to enjoy them completely, drop that parent role as often as you can so you can be a friend as well as a father or mother. This approach will bring you a wonderful new relationship with them.

16

How to Turn Off a Person's Anger Immediately

If a person is angry with you, or if he views you with suspicion and mistrust, it will usually be for one of several reasons. It could be because of something you've said or done. It might also be because of something he *thinks* you've said or done. Either way, you'll need to take some sort of corrective action to resolve this problem, even if you're not at fault.

At times, a person will take out his anger at the system—for instance, the company or corporation, the government, even society as a whole—on you only because you happen to be the closest or most convenient target. Finally, some people's imaginations work overtime. They have the idea that everybody in the whole world is against them or out to get them.

But, no matter what the cause of a person's anger is, you'll want to turn it off immediately so you can restore normal friendly relationships with him again. You can do that easily with the methods I'll give you in this chapter.

BENEFITS YOU'll GAIN

1. When you use the *White Magic* technique, you'll not only turn off a person's anger immediately, but you'll also convert him into your faithful friend and loyal supporter.

2. The second technique you'll learn will show you how to change a belligerent neighbor into a true friend.

3. The *Fact-Finder* technique will not only stop an angry

person dead in his tracks and create a friend for you, but it can also be used to improve business relationships and make more money for yourself, just as a young vitamin salesman, Sam Pierce, did.

4. You can use the *Power Play That Never Fails* to turn a recalcitrant, stubborn and mean, dissatisfied person into a cooperative, friendly individual.

5. The last technique you'll learn takes some extra special effort on your part, but it will be well worth it, for you can turn anger and bitterness into love and friendship when you use it.

TECHNIQUES YOU CAN USE TO GAIN THESE BENEFITS

One of the most distinguished Supreme Court Justices our country ever had said in effect, "To be able to listen to others in a sympathetic and understanding manner is the most effective method you can use to get along with people and tie up their friendships for good." This famous Justice went on to say that few people knew how to practice the "white magic" of being a good listener.

How You, Too, Can Practice the "White Magic" Technique

I personally have found that you can turn off a person's anger immediately if you will *simply listen to his story from beginning to end without any interruption whatever*. After he's finished, then tell him you agree with him or that 'you understand his point of view. Finally, ask him exactly what he wants you to do about it. Now let me show you how Carl Feldman, an employee relations manager, uses this technique so you can see how well it works.

"When an angry employee comes into my office, I handle him like a VIP," Carl says. "I treat him as if he were the company president or a majority stockholder. I ask him to sit down and make himself comfortable. Then I offer him a cigarette, get him a cup of coffee. I do everything I can to put him at ease.

"Then I ask him to tell me his problem. I say that I want to hear it all from beginning to end. *I listen to his story without interrupting him,* not even once. I never say a word. I just listen so he can get it all off his chest. That's what he wants; someone who'll listen to him; someone who'll lend a sympathetic ear.

"After he's through, I tell him I can really understand how he feels. I make him feel that I agree with him, even if I don't! I say that if I were in his shoes, if the situation were reversed, I'd no doubt feel the same way he does.

"Now I've already taken a lot of steam out of him just by listening to him and then by telling him I understand exactly how he feels. He wasn't at all prepared for this, so he calms down even more. Instead of finding that I'm his enemy or that I'm against him, he suddenly finds that I'm on his side and that I'm his friend. He came in all set for a big battle with me, but now he suddenly finds he has no one to fight.

"Now I add the finishing touch. *I ask him what he wants me to do about his problem.* This really floors him because ninety-five percent of the time, a manager doesn't *ask* his employee what he can do for him, he *tells* him what he's going to do.

"But we don't run our employee relations program that way. *We never tell an angry employee with a complaint what we're going to do. Instead, we always ask him what he wants us to do.*

"I've had employees look at me with open-mouthed astonishment and say, 'Gosh, Mr. Feldman, I honestly don't know. I hadn't given much thought to that at all. I just wanted someone to listen to my side of the story for a change. You've done that for me, so that's really all I want. I'm satisfied now.'

"However, sometimes they will say what they expect us to do. In most cases, I find they ask for much less than I would have offered. When I give them even more than they ask for, they are deeply impressed with the generosity of management and the company.

"Actually, my job is very easy. All I do is listen with a sympathetic ear. Then I ask the person what he wants me to do. When he tells me that, I help him get what he wants."

When you analyze this "white magic" technique, you'll see that Mr. Feldman is gaining mastery over people by finding out what they want and helping them get it. If you will remember, I said back in Chapter 1 that to find out what a person wants and help him get it is the number one rule in the mastery of people.

A Technique You Can Use to Calm Down an Angry Neighbor

When your neighbor gets angry with you, you can do one of two things: you can get mad and fight back, or you can do exactly the opposite—take steps to appease his anger.

Now if you fight back and try to retaliate—which is exactly what the other person expects you to do—you will lose complete control of the situation and only make things worse. You will accomplish absolutely nothing if you lose your temper, too. In fact, the inability to control one's temper indicates a definite lack of self-discipline. And if a person cannot master himself, he certainly cannot expect to master others.

What happens, then, if you don't fight back? Does this mean that the other individual will automatically win? Of course not. The only time you can be really sure of winning is when you don't lose your temper and retaliate. It always takes at least two people to make a fight. When you refuse to become angry, the other person's anger has to burn itself out. Let me give you an example:

"I have a next-door neighbor with a short fuse who flies off the handle for almost any reason," Kenneth N. told me. "It used to be that when he came over raising the devil about something, I'd get mad, yell back, and we'd get nowhere. We always ended up in a shouting match until I learned how to control him.

"Now when he gets mad at me—which seldom happens any more because he knows he can't win—I simply remain calm and quiet instead of flying off the handle too. When I refuse to fight, he realizes that he might as well cuss out a tree or a shrub, so he throws in the towel and gives up."

The best way to turn off your neighbor's anger immediately is to respond in a kind and friendly manner. Remain completely calm. Say nothing until he's drained himself emotionally. Then answer him quietly and softly, for as the Good Book says, "A soft answer turneth away wrath," and that's ever so true. If you use a quiet soft tone of voice, it will not only calm the other person down, but it will also keep you from getting angry as well.

When you refuse to fight back, when you hold your temper in check and speak softly, the angry person quickly realizes that he's the only one yelling. This embarrasses him and makes him feel like a fool. He will suddenly become extremely self-conscious and anxious to get the situation back to normal as soon as possible.

You can use this psychology to master and control the angry person and calm his emotions until he becomes rational and reasonable again. So, when you find yourself in a tense situation with an angry neighbor—or anyone else, for that matter—stay cool and calm. Deliberately lower your voice and keep it down. This will motivate the angry individual to lower his own voice. As long as he speaks softly, he cannot possibly remain angry and high-strung for very long.

How to Use the "Fact-Finder Technique" to Stop an Angry Person Dead in His Tracks

When a person is angry with you, it will usually be for one of several reasons. It could be because of something you've said or done. It could also be because of something he *thinks* you've said or done. Sometimes he'll take out his anger on you, even though he's upset with someone else.

No matter what the cause of his anger, and no matter who the person is—employee, customer, client, business associate, or friend—it's up to you to find out what the problem is so you can correct it and restore friendly relationships with him immediately.

The best way to do this is to use the "fact finder" technique. In other words, play cop and go after all the facts in the case just as a good detective would. Ask questions of *what...who... when...where...why...how...*until you discover what he's mad about.

Find out *why* the person is angry...*what* made him mad...are *you* responsible for doing so...if not, *who* is...*when* did it happen...*where*...*how*? Ask *what* you can do to set things straight after you find out *what* is wrong.

I always use the fact finder technique to find the reason behind a person's anger. Even when I think I have all the answers, to make absolutely certain I will still ask one more question: "Is there any other reason for you to be upset about this?" Let me show you by an example now how well this technique will work.

Sam Pierce, a young salesman for a vitamin products company, attended one of my seminars. He told me about a big account with a large health clinic that his company had lost and had not been able to regain. I suggested that he go back to call on them again and use the fact finder technique to find out what had gone wrong. About a month later, I received a letter from him. It read as follows:

"As you suggested, I went back and requested an interview with the chief administrative officer of the clinic. Our conversation went like this:

" 'Dr. Smith, my company would like to know exactly *why* we lost your business. We feel sure you must have a good reason for leaving us because no one makes a better product more economically than we do. We must have been guilty of some mistake and we'd like to know what it is so we won't make the same mistake again with somebody else. Will you please tell me what we did wrong?'

"His answer was, 'I simply decided to try a different company. I'm perfectly happy with their service and have no desire to change.'

" 'Dr. Smith, isn't there some specific reason you left us?' I asked. 'In addition to what you've told me, isn't there some other reason?'

"After a long silence, he said, 'Your company president promised me a special extra five percent discount on our purchases because of our large volume of business. But when I received your bill, it was for the full amount. There was no extra discount. I had my bookkeeping section call your accounting department to find out why. They told us the company never gave extra discounts to anyone, no matter who they were or how much they bought. So I figured I'd been lied to just to get our business so I quit your company and went somewhere else.'

"I knew there had to be a mistake somewhere so I asked Dr. Smith if I could call my office collect right then and find out where the error was. When I talked to the company president, the mistake was discovered immediately. He had simply forgotten to tell the accounting department about the special five percent discount for Dr. Smith.

"I asked him to speak with Dr. Smith right then and there so this misunderstanding could be cleared up. He did so, and as a result, we regained the biggest account our company has, all because I used your fact finder technique and refused to give up until I had all the answers."

How to Use the "Power Play" to Turn Off a Person's Anger

This is the best technique to use on a person who's angry because he feels slighted, overlooked, or left out. Basically, this person's problem is that he wants attention and he'll do almost anything to get it. Lack of attention destroys his ego and makes him feel unimportant and unwanted.

Remember that the desire to be important is a deep craving in every one of us. The best way, then, to handle the person who feels overlooked and left out is to make him feel important by paying attention to him. You can do that by asking for his help, his opinions, and his advice. This procedure will turn off a person's anger immediately and change his attitude completely around. Let me give you a concrete example:

A friend of mine, Hal Burke, a department foreman, was having all sorts of morale problems with one of his employees. "Jack's a heck of a good man," Hal told me, "and I don't want to lose him. The problem is, Jack was passed over for promotion to supervisor a couple of months ago and he's been mad ever since. He's a good man where he is, but he's reached the top level of his ability.

"Give me some ideas on how to handle him, Jim."

"Give him a job where he's noticed by others so he can feel extra important, even if it's only temporary or part-time work," I said. "For example, put him in charge of reviewing the safety regulations or inventory procedures for your department. Tell him you want his recommendations because you value his opinion highly in view of his long experiences with the company. Pay him extra if you can for this special work.

"If this isn't feasible, figure out some other special project for him to do that carries extra responsibility and high visibility. Some sort of trouble-shooting job would be perfect for him. Just make sure it's the kind of job that makes him feel important and that will cause other employees to take notice of him, too."

Did this work for Hal? Of course it did. When Jack got the feeling of importance that he needed so much, his anger evaporated and the situation returned to normal almost immediately. Once Jack's bruised ego was healed, he forgot all about the supervisory position that he'd missed out on.

This technique will work for you, too. All you need do is pay attention to the angry person who feels slighted or overlooked. Making a person feel important is a power play that never fails. It'll work every time on everyone; no exceptions.

How to Turn Off a Person's Anger and Win a Friend

To say you're sorry, even when you're wrong, seems to come hard to most people. It's hard to apologize. But when you are wrong, you ought to quickly admit it. I know of no faster or better way to turn off a person's anger and win a true friend than to apologize to the individual whose feelings you've hurt.

I once had occasion to write to a lawyer with whom I was extremely unhappy. I felt that the fee he'd charged me was far too high, and I told him so. I guess I got carried away for my letter became more caustic than I'd meant for it to be.

He called me to tell me in no uncertain terms what he thought of both me and my remarks. He was really angry and he laid it on hot and heavy. When he finally paused for breath, I cut in and said, "Brad, I'm truly sorry I wrote that letter in such haste. I should never have done so. I apologize for what I said. You have a perfect right to be upset. Please forgive me."

He was quiet for a moment and then he said, "That's okay, Jim. I admire you for having the courage to say you're wrong and apologize. Maybe my fee was a bit high, so I guess I owe you an apology, too. I'll send you a new one. Let's be friends and start all over, okay?"

So you see, to promptly admit your mistake when you're wrong and apologize to the person you've hurt can immediately turn his anger into a lasting friendship. But you can go even further than that for even better results.

All you need do is to say you're sorry even when you're not at fault. When you're not in the wrong, you can afford to be big about things. If just saying you're sorry will restore peace in the family, or restore friendly relationships between two people, then say it so you can get on with the more important business of enjoying each other's companionship, rather than worrying and fretting about who's right or wrong.

How to Master the Art of Getting Ahead in Today's Business World

To be able to get ahead in today's business world, you must know how to master people and solve people problems. You see, it isn't problems with profit, sales, or production that cause all your headaches in business. It's people and people problems.

For example, you can solve your profit problems with better control over costs and expenditures. You can solve your sales problems and gain more customers with better sales techniques and procedures. And you can handle your production problems by more efficient methods, eliminating wasted motion and duplication of effort, improving the quality, cutting out excess waste, and numerous other ways.

But even when you solve all these problems, you are still going to find yourself with people problems, for *people are needed to solve those profit, sales, and production problems*. You'll always need people to help you become successful in the business world, for you can't possibly do it all by yourself.

That's why this specific chapter is so valuable to you, for it will give you specific techniques you can use to master people and to control and direct their activities so you can get ahead and become an outstanding success in the business world.

THE BIG BENEFITS YOU'LL GAIN FROM THIS CHAPTER

1. *You'll Make Much Money.* Ever since the Phoenicians invented money several thousand years ago, the primary aim of

every person has been to make as much of it as possible. This chapter will show you how to guide and direct the activities of people in the business world so you can go ahead and make more of it.

2. *You'll Have Great Power over Others* when you become a success in business. You'll find that your influence will expand outward and you can become the leader, not only in business activities, but also in social, political, and community affairs as well.

3. *Personal Power, Prestige, Respect and Recognition Will All Be Yours* along with your financial success when you become a prosperous businessperson.

4. *You Can Use Your Mastery over People to Succeed in Business.* For example, if you're a secretary, you can develop your own power tactics to master your boss and move up the business ladder of success. If you're now at the bottom in a big company, you can use those same tactics to move up to top management and executive levels. No matter who you are, what you do, or how low your position is right now, you can use your personal power tactics to master people so that every success you ever dreamed of can be yours.

TECHNIQUES YOU CAN USE TO GAIN THESE MARVELOUS BENEFITS

How a Secretary Mastered Her Boss to Climb the Business Ladder to Success·

The first thing you must realize as a secretary is that *no one is interested in your success but you.* To tell you the straight unvarnished truth, your own boss is the last person in the entire organization who wants to see you get ahead. Do you know why? Because he doesn't want to lose you, that's why. If he loses you, he has to start all over again, educating and training a new secretary to do the work the way he wants it done. So, the first point to keep in mind is *not* to be the "perfect" secretary, but to be the "almost perfect" secretary.

1. *Attract the Attention of the Upper Hierarchy.* Although you

do want to keep your boss happy with you and your work, your primary objective must be to get ahead. If you are a secretary, the best way for you to move up the ladder is to become known to your superior's boss as a knowledgeable and competent individual who really knows the workings of the organization inside out.

Let me show you now by an example how to do exactly that:

Charlene Mason is today the Chief Administrative Staff Officer for a large corporation. She reports directly to the president of the company; to no one else. She has custody of important documents and corporation books, submits reports and statements to state and federal governments, is in charge of the transfer of corporate stock, and sees that the minutes of stockholders' meetings are properly kept and recorded. She has a large staff of her own to help her carry out these various duties. Yet Charlene started out as a file clerk for a department foreman away down on the totem pole.

"I didn't want to be a file clerk all my life, so I formulated my own plan of attack and my own timetable for success," Charlene says. "The first thing I knew I had to do was attract the attention of those who counted. And I don't mean by wearing low-cut revealing blouses and hip-hugging skirts either.

"Except for ordinary reports and routine memos, I quickly learned to keep important correspondence and major reports out of the interoffice mail. When I saw that a letter or a report was of significant nature, I would suggest to my boss that I hand-carry it to his superior. Of course, I would always imply that this would make my own boss look good.

"Once in his superior's office, I would bypass his secretary by saying, 'Mr. Black asked me to personally give this report to Mr. Green.' I wouldn't just lay it down on Mr. Green's desk and then leave. Instead, I would hand it to him and say, 'This is the report on production you've been waiting for from Mr. Black. I'll be glad to stay for a moment so if you have any questions I can answer them for you.'

"I always made it very clear that I understood the report and that I knew what it was all about. Before long, Mr. Green got in the habit of telling his own secretary to 'Call Charlene and ask her; she'll know.' When his own secretary got married and left, he didn't look around to find a replacement. He immediately tagged me and I took my first step up the ladder.

"But I didn't stay put in Mr. Green's office. That was only an intermediate goal. I used the same process, with a few slight variations, to come up to where I am today."

2. *Become the Fountainhead of Information and Knowledge.* Just as Charlene did, you will attract the attention of the people who count when you fill yourself with accurate and useful information. The more knowledge you display, the more people will turn to you to find out what they need to know.

The more information you gain about the entire operation, that much more will your boss depend on you for answers. It will soon reach the point where he won't go to a staff meeting without you. When he turns to you for an answer when the president of the company asks him a question, guess whose name is going to be remembered.

Let me tell you how I used this technique successfully when I was in the army during World War II. I was a sergeant. I had a major for a boss. As a regimental staff officer, he attended division staff meetings on a weekly basis. Since he was hard of hearing, he almost always came back with unintelligible notes. I suggested to him that I attend the meetings with him and take notes for him.

High-ranking division officers got used to seeing a sergeant come with the major to take notes and answer questions. One day the Commanding General attended the meeting. I saw that he watched me intently and asked several other officers why I was there. After the meeting was over, I was directed to report to his office.

"You shouldn't be an enlisted man," he told me. "You should be an officer. You're already performing the duties of a major, but you're only receiving the pay of a sergeant. I'm recommending you immediately for a field promotion to first lieutenant."

Sixty days later, I was commissioned an officer in the United States Army without having to endure the physical and mental stresses of thirteeen weeks of Infantry Officer Candidate School.

3. *Never Come Early, but Always Stay Late.* If you show up early, the only people who'll ever see you are the janitor or the mailroom clerk. Neither one of them can help you get promoted.

Never, and I repeat never, leave before your boss does. If you do, it will never fail but that he will want you that particular day. Always, and again, I repeat, always, leave after your boss does.

He'll be impressed with your loyalty to the company and your devotion to duty.

If at all possible, try to time your departure to that of *his* boss. The more his boss sees of you, the more he will remember you. Carry some trade journals under your arm so he can see how interested you are in your profession. But don't carry anything that suggests you're doing your office work at home. This gives him the impression that you're not efficient enough to get your work done during regular working hours.

4. *Eat Your Lunch at Your Desk.* You don't have to do this every day; several times a week will do. This also implies great devotion to duty and never fails to create a good impression. But don't read a newspaper or magazine or do your face or nails at your desk during the lunch hour. This spoils the effect you're trying to create. Instead, open a file or a report. If your boss wants to know why you're not going out to eat lunch, tell him that you want to absorb the details of this complicated report while everyone's gone and it's peaceful and quiet.

Don't worry that people will think you're cheap or antisocial when you brown bag it. You're in good company when you do. Leon Peters, Chairman of the Board of Cushman and Wakefield Realtors and consultant to RCA, does this, and so do many other top executives. They can get much of their most important work done when most of the office staff is out and there isn't much chance for telephone interruptions.

5. *Look as if You Were Already a Top-Level Executive.* I am not going into the details of how you should dress. That depends entirely on where you live and what the dress code and customs are for your company. The important thing is for you to show those above you that you will fit in perfectly well at their level.

6. *If You Can't Go Up Vertically, Move Laterally.* It will sometimes happen that no matter what you do, you won't be able to move up where you are. In that case, move laterally from one job to another. You'll not only learn much more about the company, but you will also sooner or later find the right slot where you can move up the ladder.

If anyone higher up wonders about your horizontal movements, you can always say that you want to get the broadest education possible about all departments in the company so you will be better qualified. This always impresses the hierarchy. They'll remember your name when the right time comes.

How You Can Get Ahead in the Big Company

Everything I've just said about how a secretary can climb the business ladder to success applies also to the person who is just entering the lowest level of management. However, the rest of this particular section will be aimed specifically at management. But if you're a secretary, that doesn't mean you shouldn't read it. After all, plenty of top-level women executives started out as secretaries or file clerks. Remember that Charlene Mason did.

1. *Never Make an Issue of Small Matters.* Go along with minor or insignificant points when you can do so without causing damage to yourself or to your own position. When you do have to make an issue of something, be sure it is a major point. Then your objection will stand out and you'll be remembered and well thought of for your professional attitude and conduct.

2. *State Your Objection Calmly and Courteously.* If you disagree with a major point, back up that disagreement with logic, reason, and facts. Objections based on emotion or on how you "feel" about something won't carry much weight. If the final decision goes against your recommendation, don't carry a chip on your shoulder. Do your level best to support the selected course of action of your superior. You'll be highly respected when you do.

3. *Develop the "Golden Touch" in Human Relationships.* The ability to get along with others is an absolute must if you want to get ahead in the big corporation. You cannot move up the ladder of success if you make an enemy out of everyone. In fact, knowing how to handle people is one of the hallmarks of executive leadership. If you can't get along well with your associates, if you are constantly involved in verbal warfare with someone, you'll be let go, no matter what your qualifications and ability.

4. *Be Enthusiastic About Your Job.* Don't expect to move up the management ladder if you don't really have your heart in your work. Your boss can tell, for your attitude will be reflected on your face and in your actions.

If you can't go to work smiling because you love your job, I really feel sorry for you. I would suggest that you get enthusiastic about your work or that you change jobs before it's too late.

5. *Don't Be Afraid to Take a Reasonable Risk.* Top-level executives expect their management people to have the courage to take reasonable risks. If you always play it safe, you'll never get anywhere. Good prior planning will prevent most major problems and greatly reduce the risks involved for you.

6. *Look for More Responsibility.* The person who ducks responsibility will never go to the top. Upper-level executives are always on the lookout for those who can accept more and more responsibility. The person who can is always labeled as a "comer."

Remember that every time you delegate a job to someone else to do, you're not passing the buck. Instead, you're freeing yourself to accept additional responsibility. Top management is always extremely happy to find a competent individual who is available to take care of new projects. If you want to climb the management ladder and achieve success, then let that person be you.

7. *Dream Up Your Own Technique for Advancement.* Jerry L. used one of the cleverest techniques I've ever seen to climb the management ladder to success. Shortly after he went to work for a large company, Jerry realized that promotion was going to be a slow process. Then he had a brilliant flash of inspiration.

One of his college friends had gone to work for an executive recruiting firm. He, too, was anxious to succeed. Jerry gave his boss's name to his friend, who was able to entice him away from the firm. Jerry then moved into his boss's slot. He used the same procedure several times to reach his present position in top-level management, leaving behind others with more seniority and experience.

How to Go into Business for Yourself and Be Successful

If you will recall, I told you in Chapter 1 that small businesses that failed didn't determine what people's needs were before they started. But successful individuals in business found out what their customers wanted before they ever opened the door.

So, if you want to go into business for yourself, then you ought to do the same thing. Find out what people want before you start.

Then help them get it. When you use that procedure, you are bound to be successful. Let me give you an example so you can see for yourself exactly how one person did this:

Bill Wilson, a successful businessman, owner of a local water service with two customer service centers, and employer of twenty-eight people, followed these same basic principles to start his own company.

Bill came to Florida to live after leaving the military. He wanted to go into business for himself rather than work for someone else, but he was not completely sure of what kind to go into.

Before he made that vital decision, he decided to make a survey of the area so he could find out what people wanted or what essential service was lacking. He went from house to house, knocked on hundreds of doors, and talked to a tremendous number of people to get his answer.

Bill found that the majority of people complained about the high cost of using city water to keep their yards beautiful and green. You see, in spite of all its lakes and being surrounded by water on three sides, Florida never has enough rainfall. Grass must be watered constantly throughout the year or lawns will die out and become nothing but barren weed patches.

Based on his survey to find out what people wanted, Bill made the decision to go into the lawn sprinkling business. He digs a deep well so the home owner has a source of free water for his lawn that he never has to pay for again. Then he puts in a yard-watering system complete with pump, undergound pipes, and lawn sprinklers.

Another major complaint that people had was the extremely hard city water that corroded plumbing fixtures, ruined washing machines and dishwashers, made clothes take on a dirty gray and grimy look, and left a filthy ring that could never be completely removed from the tub after a bath. So Bill also installs water conditioning units that convert the hard city water to soft gentle water that no longer corrodes expensive plumbing fixtures or ruins washing machines and dishwashers as well as good clothing.

Bill is successful because he found out what people wanted before he started his business. Then he went all out to help them get what they wanted. He believes fully that total service to the customer is the real key to business success. Bill says that the customer comes first, last, and always, for without customers, there is no business.

If you will follow Bill's method of finding out what people want so you can help them get it, and practice his philosophy of total dedication and service to the customer, you can't help but succeed no matter what business you go into. It will be absolutely impossible for you to fail.

How to Handle Other Members of the "Power Elite"— and Come Out on Top

Perhaps you might not yet be in the position to work with top-level members of the "power elite," but the time will definitely come when you will be *if you prepare yourself now.*

Don't imagine for a moment that the top-level members of the power elite who inhabit the executive suite are anxious to see you succeed. They are not. In fact, just the opposite is true. Just as the secretary in the last chapter found out, you, too, will discover that *no one is interested in your success except you, and you alone.*

Even the most efficient top-level executive will view each newcomer with suspicion and as a possible threat to him and to his position. If necessary, he will stop at nothing to protect his job and his way of life. If he feels that you are a menace to him in any way, he will go all out to get rid of you, no matter what your qualifications and abilities are.

So, your first rule of survival in the executive suite is to be on guard at all times. If you will learn to use the techniques of attack and defense that I'll give you in this chapter, you will be able to master and control the members of the power elite—and come out on top.

BENEFITS YOU'LL GAIN FROM THIS CHAPTER

1. *You Can Go Clear to the Very Top.* When you know how to handle the top-level people in the power structure, there is

absolutely no limit to how far you can go. You can become president of the company or even chairman of the board if that's what you really want and are willing to go after it. It's all up to you, for you can gain whatever goal you want to achieve.

2. *You'll Gain Great Power over Others.* When you learn how to master and control the members of the power elite, you'll gain great power over people. They'll have to provide you with whatever you want from them. You'll receive offers of business deals, social honors, positions of community leadership that command respect. Even your "enemies" in the executive suite will approach you; actually want to work with you; want to do favors for you; make special offers to you.

3. *You'll Gain a Success You Only Dreamed of Before.* As a member of the power elite who knows how to handle others of that group, you'll achieve a degree of personal success greater than any you've ever experienced before. Prestige, power, respect, influence, recognition, more success than you ever thought possible—all these will be yours.

TECHNIQUES YOU CAN USE TO GAIN THESE POWERFUL BENEFITS

How to Read the "Invisible" Company Power Chart

Every company or corporation has two power charts. The official one shows the line-and-staff organization structure. This chart is described in an organization manual, usually called an SOP (Standing Operating Procedure). Formal power and authority lines are clearly shown. It is available for anyone to read and study.

The unofficial power chart is invisible. You can't find it on paper so you can study it, but it's still there. You can understand this chart only by constant and careful observation. Since this is the real power chart, it will affect promotions and raises, resignations and dismissals.

The power lines in the invisible chart are formed by office politics. If you want to get ahead and stay there, you must thoroughly study and understand this invisible but very real power chart. Let me show you some of the things to watch for. You may find others in your particular organization, but the points I will give you are usually common to all companies.

1. *Who Is the Real Information Source?* Rumors and gossip often flow rampant through all levels of the organization. However, dependable information will normally come from someone who sets policy or makes decisions, or from an individual close to him.

This does not necessarily mean that the person in authority on the official power chart will make the final decision on a crucial matter. It's up to you to find out who the real power source is; who's behind the scenes pulling the strings.

2. *Who in the Organization Socializes with the Power Elite?* People who work together do not always play together. Most social relationships are established by membership in some organization outside the company. The connection can be political, religious, even athletic. It can result from lodge or club membership. It may also be a result of the social standing of one's spouse. Whatever the relationship is, it gives that person an edge on power and an "in" with those who count. Be smart; know who all these people are. Keep your guard up and watch your tongue at all times when around them.

3. *Find Out Which Employee Has Real Authority in the Invisible Power Line.* It can come as a complete surprise to you to find that someone outside the official power line has the authority to either okay or kill a project. Without his initials of approval, a proposal or recommendation will die.

When I first went to work as a junior executive with a big company, I submitted a recommendation to my superior for cutting production costs in a particular department. "Take it to B.J.," he said. "Get his approval first."

"B.J." I said, surprised at his remark. "Why? He doesn't have any authority whatever in this area."

"You're wrong," my boss said. "B.J. doesn't have any 'official' authority in any specific area, but he's been here since the place first opened. The boss values his judgment highly. Without his initials of approval on your proposal, your recommendation won't get anywhere."

4. *Who's Related to Whom in the Power Structure?* These people have an "in" simply because of a blood tie or a marriage

relationship. If two people are equal in qualifications and ability, but one of them is the boss's nephew or his wife's cousin, guess who's going to be promoted when only one opening is available. Keep a good weather eye on relatives of any kind. They may be powerless today, but have great power and authority tomorrow, even though it could be a "borrowed" power, a point I'll discuss later.

How to Project Your Personal Power at This Level

You can use a variety of methods to subtly project your personal power so it will leave a definite impression on other members of the power elite.

1. *How to Create Your Own "Space Bubble."* In companies and corporations the general rule of thumb is that the more powerful you become, the larger the area you can call your own. Low-ranked employees may work together in groups in one large room. The supervisor might have only a glassed-in cubicle from which he can both see and be seen by his subordinates.

A young executive can be blessed with a private, although small, office. As a member of the power elite, even if you're a junior one, you should be entitled to that.

No matter how small your office is, you can expand your own space bubble of power by placing visitors' chairs against the farthest wall as far away as possible from your desk. Another person should never be able to *invade* or *encroach* upon your territory by putting his arms on your desk.

2. *What to Do About Names and Titles.* Never refer to yourself by your first name. If you call someone on the phone, don't say, "This is Joe." Don't even say, "This is Joe Horner." Instead, just say, "This is Horner." The use of first names encourages familiarity. In power elite circles, familiarity is an invasion of privacy. It punctures your space bubble. Be courteous and polite, of course, but keep people at arm's length.

When answering the phone, don't use your title. Don't say, "This is *Mr.* Horner, or *Superintendent* Horner, or *Doctor, Professor, Major,* or whatever. Just say, "Horner," or "Horner speaking." When introducing yourself to someone, say, "I'm Horner," or "My name is Horner."

If you are a woman, follow exactly the same procedure. This places you on the same level as your male associates. Never refer to yourself as *Miss, Ms.,* or *Mrs.* This invites too many chauvinistic jokes, especially about the title, *Ms.*

Why is all this so important? Because people who depend on titles are using *borrowed power* to get by on. They have no real personal power of their own.

3. *Eliminate These Words from Your Vocabulary.* Certain words and phrases automatically place other people above you when you use them. You can bring yourself up to their level immediately by eliminating these words completely from your vocabulary.

I refer specifically to the use of the words "Sir" and "Ma'am." Never use these words either alone or in the phrases so often heard: "Yes, sir," "No, sir," "Yes, ma'am, "No, ma'am."

The use of *sir* and *ma'am* immediately places you on a lower level than the other person whether you realize it or not. These two small words imply *submissiveness* rather than courtesy and respect. You can still be courteous without being submissive. For example, if your boss asks if you've completed a certain task, don't answer with "Yes, sir." Just say, "Yes, Mr. Jones, I have."

Don't reply with only *yes* or *no* when answering a question. It sounds too curt and brief. Answer *yes* or *no* in a short sentence just as I showed you in the paragraph above. If the person to whom you are speaking has a title, use that, too. For instance, you can say, "Yes, Doctor, I have," "No, Major, I have not."

How to Use "Silent Power Cues" to Project Your Personal Charisma and Magnetism

Silent power cues are body gestures and posture; facial movements and expressions; staring down the other person making a power play. I want to cover each of these now in detail.

1. *How to Use Body Gestures and Posture to Project Power.* I already told you in a previous chapter how powerful people could use the "steepling technique" to project power. Another way to project power by your posture is to appear relaxed and at ease.

For example, in an interview the power person is relaxed and at ease in his posture. He can choose to stand, sit, even stroll around. If a man, he might straddle a chair or put his feet up on the desk. If a woman, she could place her hands on her hips to project power. The person being interviewed is powerless; he can do none of these.

2. *How to Use Your Eyes to Project Your Power*. A powerful person is accustomed to staring down another individual as a way of invading his territory. There's a trick to this. Never stare directly into the other person's eyes. Pick a spot in the middle of his forehead just above the level of the eyebrows. Keep your eyes glued to that spot and no one can ever stare you down.

3. *How Your Facial Expression Can Display Power*. You can also project power by maintaining a neutral facial expression. At a high-level meeting of business executives, the ranking individual rarely smiles, even when greeted cordially by others. Less powerful people smile throughout the entire meeting.

Let me sum up the importance of using silent power cues to project your personal charisma and magnetism this way: You can use nonverbal language either to project your superiority to a subordinate or to communicate your equality with your associates without ever saying a word. Silence in itself is one of the most potent nonverbal signs of power you can ever use.

How to Control the Person Who Uses "Borrowed Power" to Get By

The person who uses "borrowed power," trying to influence and direct the actions of others, has no real personal power of his own. Borrowed power is agency power. Even though that person can use agency power to his advantage, the power does not come from him.

For example, in the military services, people who use borrowed power to get what they want will usually be generals' aides and high-ranking officers' wives. In business, it can be the boss's secretary, a brother-in-law, nephew, or some other relative.

You can easily identify people with agency or borrowed power this way. They have nothing to offer to get what they're after. They always try to get what they want without fulfilling another person's needs. Since they have no real personal power to achieve their goals, they have to use the position or status of others who do have the power. In short, they are parasites. They always try to get something for nothing, usually by using veiled threats.

Another trick that people with borrowed power will try is to issue an order they are not authorized to give. The recipient of such an order will attempt to carry it out and then end up in a peck of trouble when he does so. This is often what the person with borrowed power wants to have happen.

You can usually recognize at once whether an order is legitimate or not by what you hear. If you hear phrases like, "This is what the boss wants," "This is what the boss asked for," "This is what the general manager told me to do," watch out. In the end, when something goes wrong, it will be only your word against his.

The best way to keep this from happening to you is to follow one simple rule: *Never take orders from anyone outside of your power line of authority.* If your boss tells you to do it, then do it. If *his* boss tells you to do it, do it. But if you're in personnel, and someone in purchasing or sales or engineering tells you to do it, forget it. Tell him to run it through proper command channels if he wants it done.

When you know from experience how people use agency or borrowed power to gain their ends, you'll know how to defend yourself. Some people will foolishly defer to those with borrowed power, primarily because of their fear that they could lose their position or status if they don't.

Always be courteous, of course, but simply refuse to do their bidding. As soon as you stand your ground, the person with borrowed power will leave you alone. Give in and you'll be under his thumb forever. Remember that when the present power structure changes, people with borrowed power will be the first to go. When their source of power disappears, so will they. And so might you, if you've been catering to them.

How to Master and Control the Person with Real Power

It is far easier to master and control the person with real power than the person who uses agency or borrowed power. People with real power are those who really count in the long run. They'll be around long after those with agency or borrowed power are gone.

All you need do is practice the basic premise I've stressed over and over again from the beginning of this book. That is simply to...

Find out what the other person wants so you can help him get it.

How Can You Find Out What He Wants? Get a little black notebook and keep your eyes and ears open so you can gather and record intelligence information about those individuals who are important to you and to your career. Use the fourteen basic needs and desires every normal person has as your guide for gathering useful information about your target.

Now don't get the wrong idea here. The data you record in your notebook is not to be used for blackmail purposes. You are gathering information only to find out what the other person wants so you can help him get it.

No doubt, the two key individuals who are vital to your success are your own boss and, in turn, his boss. So, find out everything you can about them: their likes and dislikes; their odd quirks and idiosyncrasies; their customs and habits; their strong points and their weak ones.

How You Can Help Him Get What He Wants. Once you know what your boss likes, help him get it. If he's a bug about getting reports in early, then get them in early. If he wants his desk completely cleared off by quitting time, then help him by getting that done. If he frowns on people coming in late, then never be late. Whatever he wants, help him get it. After all, he's the one you want to keep happy and contented.

I do want to stress that while you are creating a strong alliance with your boss and with his boss by making sure they get what they want, don't make enemies out of those who can't do anything for you at the moment.

Things always change. Promotion, retirement, death, dismissal, transfer, any of these can change the status quo in a moment, so always be prepared for any eventuality. No matter what happens in the circles of the power elite, be ready to jump in any direction and you'll always come out on top.

19

The Secret Leverage
That Gives You Control
over Problem People

I touched upon the subject of problem people in Chapter 8, where I discussed how you could become a master trouble-shooter by helping people solve their problems. Here, I want to expand that discussion for problem people who require special methods and need extra attention because they are either potential or actual troublemakers. They can destroy good friendly relationships and create havoc in any group.

Every factory and store, church and club, community and neighborhood, always has a certain percentage of problem people. If these individuals are allowed to go their own willful way unchecked, they can cause a great deal of harm or damage.

In previous books, I covered in great detail the troubles that problem people can create in business. I will also cover these points here, but not in as much detail, for this is not a book written primarily for executives, managers, and supervisors.

This is a book written expressly for everyone who wants to gain power and mastery over others, so I have expanded the scope of problem people to the neighborhood and the residential community.

If you do want to delve deeper into the discussion of problem people in business and industry, then I would recommend that you read the following books: *Guide to Managing People, The 22 Biggest Mistakes Managers Make and How to Correct Them,* and *Van Fleet's Master Guide for Managers.* These are all published by Parker

Publishing Company, West Nyack, New York. The first two titles are also available in inexpensive paperback editions.

Right now you might not have any subordinates under you, and therefore, no problem people to bother you. However, the best time to learn how to handle problem people is before you have them working for you, not afterward.

Not only that, the information in this chapter can help you from being bullied by a domineering fellow worker. I know for sure that he can be a definite problem to you. Then there's where you live to consider. If you have a problem person in your neighborhood—and what residential community doesn't have at least one or two—you can use some of the techniques in this chapter to take care of him (or her), too.

BENEFITS YOU CAN GAIN FROM THIS CHAPTER

1. *You'll Convert a Problem Person into a Satisfied Worker*. If this problem person works for you, you'll want to do something positive to protect your investment of time, money, and training. If you don't, you'll end up as the military services do, replacing a person every two or three years. Few companies can afford a personnel turnover like that, for they can't train skilled replacements at taxpayers' expense as the armed services do.

2. *You Can Establish Cordial Relationships with Those Around You*. You can use the techniques in this chapter to influence a difficult boss to give you a raise, promotion and authority, status and prestige. Or you can establish harmonious and friendly relationships with a recalcitrant and sullen co-worker. You can even transform that grouchy and irritable next-door neighbor into a friendly human being by making an extra effort with him.

3. *You'll Have a Feeling of Tremendous Self-Accomplishment*, for learning how to master difficult or problem people is almost like taking a postgraduate course in applied psychology or human relations. You'll learn new and exciting techniques to master and control the problem person.

4. *You'll Broaden Beyond Measure Your Abilities to Master and Control All Kinds of People*. You can use the techniques in this chapter to put tough bosses, stubborn authorities, obstinate

customers and clients, and any other problem people in their proper places. In fact, you'll develop a sixth sense that will help you scare off a nasty person before he can cause trouble for you. As you progress in your ability to master and control problem persons, you'll develop the skills to get things done through people you never dreamed possible before.

TECHNIQUES YOU CAN USE TO GAIN THESE TERRIFIC BENEFITS

How to Identify and Isolate the Problem Person

It's important, first of all, that you know how to determine whether a person actually is or is not a real problem to you. A lot of people will disagree on this basic point. Some will say that a problem person is a nonconformist, an offbeat individual who speaks, thinks, or acts differently than the majority of people do. Others will say he's even abnormal or maladjusted. Most people tend to classify an individual with long hair or a beard as a problem.

Members of an unorthodox religious group are often regarded as being out of step with society. Mormons were once looked upon that way. Now they're considered to be a very respectable church. Today, the born-again Christian is thought to be a bit odd. But in a few years, he'll lose that tag of nonconformity.

So you see, a person could fit into any of these categories and still not be a problem to you or anyone else. As Thoreau once said, "If a man does not keep pace with his companions, perhaps it is because he hears a different drummer. Let him step to the music which he hears, however measured or far away."

No matter what other people say about a person, you need answer only one question to determine whether he's a problem to you or not. *Is this person causing you damage or harm in some way?* If he is, then he's a problem to you and you should do something to correct this situation. But if he's not causing you tangible harm or damage, *no matter what his appearance, dress, or personal behavior,* then you don't have a problem person on your hands, after all, so you need do absolutely nothing about him.

Don't let personal dislikes or prejudices about red hair, short skirts, pipe-smoking, or beards and mustaches mislead you. If you do that, you're trying to judge all people by your standards of what's right and wrong.

When you understand this simple concept of what a problem person really is, you're actually much better informed in this business of handling problem people than are a lot of personnel managers or industrial relations people who make this a full-time job.

How the Problem Person Can Create Trouble for You at Work

When you know exactly what to look for, it's very easy to identify the problem person who works for you. To cause you harm or damage at work, he must be hurting your production, your sales, or your profit. All you need do is ask yourself three simple questions. If you cannot answer *yes* to at least one of them, then he's not a problem; you'll have to look elsewhere.

1. *Is His Job Performance Below Your Standards?* Is the person's work below the accepted norm in both quality and quantity? Does he produce fewer units than he should in an average work day? Does he have more work rejected by quality control than anyone else? Does he always have fewer sales than other salespeople at the end of the week? *Does this individual fail in some specific way to measure up to the reasonable performance standards you've set and that all others are able to meet?* If he does, then he's costing you money and you definitely have a problem person on your hands.

2. *Does he Interfere with the Performance of Others?* Is this person a constant source of irritation, annoyance, or interference? Do you usually find him at the bottom of employee disturbances? Does he keep other people from doing their best work? Does the quality or the quantity of his work slow down or prevent other sections or groups from functioning properly? Does he cause some of his co-workers to lose incentive pay by his careless actions? If so, then this person is a definite problem to you.

3. *Does He Cause Harm to the Group as a Whole?* The reputation or good name of any group can be damaged even if only one of its members is a chronic source of trouble. He can keep the rest of his group constantly on edge by what he says or does. For instance, if one member of a professional athletic team gets out of

line, he gives the entire team a morale problem. One troublesome sales representative can give the entire company a bad name. If any of your people have constantly caused you to get complaints, have orders cancelled, or lose good customers by carelessness, indifference, or sloppy work, you have a problem person to take care of.

To quickly sum up this section on how to decide whether a person is actually causing you trouble or not, ask yourself these questions:

1. Is his job performance below company standards?
2. Does he interfere with the work of others?
3. Does he cause harm to his group as a whole?

If you answer *yes* to any of these three questions, you have a problem person on your hands.

How to Uncover the Cause of His Problem

It's important for you to find the real reason behind what a person says or does so you can help him solve his problem. *When his problem is solved, then yours will go away.* In other words, the best way for you to solve your problem is to help him solve his problem.

You can best do this by skillfully asking questions and carefully listening to the answers. You'll need to listen between the lines, too, for many times what a person does *not* say will tell you much more than what he does say. This is not done in a formal interview from behind a desk. Your information should be subtly gathered over a period of time by informal chats, routine visits to work sites, a cup of coffee together, that sort of thing.

I have found from personal experience that the failure of an employer or a manager to fulfill his employees' or his subordinates' basic needs on the job causes more problems than anything else. For example, if you are in charge of people, do your level best to help them achieve their desires. Here are nine specific ways you can do that:

1. Give them full credit and recognition for the work they do.
2. Make sure their work is interesting and worth while.
3. Offer them a fair wage with salary increases.
4. Give them full attention. Show that you appreciate them.

5. Promote by merit, not by seniority alone.

6. Offer them counsel on personal problems *if they ask you to*.

7. Make sure they have decent physical working conditions.

8. Within reasonable limits, offer them total job security.

9. Do anything and everything you can to make them feel important, both to you and to themselves.

When you do this, you'll have few, if any, problem persons left to deal with. Fulfilling a person's basic needs and desires gives you the *secret leverage of control* you need to get rid of ninety-nine percent of your problem people.

One last point well worth considering under the cause of problems is this: Most people resent rules and regulations that restrict their freedom and liberties. To remove that yoke of authority that problem people, as well as others, resent so much, follow this simple principle: *Rule by work; don't work by rules*. This formula will work like magic for you.

How Some Bosses Create Their Own Problems with Their People

A great many times the boss is his own biggest problem. I want to give you a list of the most common gripes people have against their bosses so you can avoid making these same mistakes when you are the boss.

I'm just going to list these complaints to you. I'm not going to give you any solutions for them. By now you've received enough information about how to master people to formulate your own answers to these problems.

1. "My boss treats me like a piece of office equipment. He makes me feel stupid in front of others. He has absolutely no knowledge whatever of human relationships."

2. "He's always making promises to get people to do things for him, but then he never keeps his word."

3. "My boss isn't fair. He plays favorites and they're the ones who get the promotions, pay raises, and special privileges. With him it isn't what you know, but who you are that counts."

4. "He never says thanks or gives a compliment to anyone.

It'd be nice to hear him say just once in a while what a good job I've done for him."

5. "He's really disorganized. Tells you something one day and then denies he ever said it the next day. You never know which way you're going with him."

6. "He always passes the buck to someone else when he makes a mistake. He wants all the credit when the job is done right, but he won't accept any of the blame when things go wrong."

7. "He discriminates against older people and women."

8. "My boss doesn't have the courage to stand for what he knows to be right. He waffles all over the place trying to compromise and please everybody."

9. "He doesn't tell the truth. You can't trust what he says."

10. "He's two-faced. Tells me what a good job I'm doing, and then tells others I'm the worst secretary he's ever had!"

How to Handle the Problem of the Neighborhood Gossip

Unfortunately, every neighborhood has at least one motor-mouth who is a potential or an actual troublemaker. A neighborhood gossip tries to demean people by spreading gossip, lies, and rumors that will blacken a person's good name and reputation or cut down his accomplishments or abilities.

Most people in the neighborhood know the gossip for what he or she really is. But sometimes they can't help but wonder if what's being said is true or not. If someone tells you some juicy tidbit about Henry or Mabel or Diane behind their backs, rest assured you are not immune to this kind of slander. That same person will talk to them about you behind your back.

You can deal with this neighborhood gossip by telling him that you are not interested in what he's saying and refuse to listen. Tell him to take his garbage somewhere else, preferably to the trash dump. If that doesn't work, then use the *silent treatment*. Don't speak to that person at all at any time.

Whether you run into the person at social activities, in business, at church, or in the supermarket, put yourself above him. Don't even say "Hello" to him. Ignore him utterly and completely.

Nothing stills a rumormonger's evil tongue more quickly than your refusal to talk with him or even listen to him. If no one will listen, how can he spread gossip and evil rumors?

We had a neighborhood gossip who was squelched by our ignoring her completely. Three of us made a solemn pact never to speak to her again. Soon our avoidance of her spread through the entire neighborhood until she was completely isolated from the whole community. How effective is this technique? It will work better than trying to fight back. Yesterday I saw a "For Sale" sign go up in front of her house.

What To Do About the Vengeful and Spiteful Vicious Neighbor

Sometimes a small problem between neighbors will erupt into open warfare. A friend of mine, Lewis P., told me about a situation like that that happened to him once.

"My backyard neighbor planted a row of oleanders along his rear boundary line," Lew said. "Trouble was, he didn't keep them trimmed and the branches kept interfering when I mowed my lawn. I have a riding mower and the oleander branches would catch the deck handle and lower the deck until I was scalping my grass. I wouldn't notice that because I was too busy dodging branches, for oleanders are deadly poisonous in spite of their beauty.

"I told my neighbor about the problem and asked him to trim the branches back, but he said his wife didn't want him to. I told him that I had no other choice than to trim them myself and that I had a legal right to do that since they were leaning over on my side of the property line.

"Unfortunately, this so enraged his wife that she nearly went crazy seeking revenge. For instance, we came back from Orlando one day after visiting our children to find a dozen limbs from a beautiful bottle brush tree in our backyard chopped off and lying on the ground. The last straw was finding the main trunk of a young live oak tree cut exactly in two. It was only five feet tall, for it was just two years old. When she finished with it, it was barely two and a half feet high.

"I went to them and asked if they'd seen anyone in my backyard while we were gone. Of course the answer was 'No.' I knew she had damaged my trees but I couldn't prove it. So to protect myself from further incursions I built a six-foot-high cypress fence across the back.

"I thought that this would solve the problem, but unfortunately it did not. I have flowering jasmine vines all over the front and one side of my house. After returning from a two-week trip, I noticed a lot of dead leaves among the vines. Investigation revealed that sixteen main leaders had been neatly cut in two.

"Again, I couldn't prove a thing, but I knew who was responsible. I called my neighbor on the phone and said, 'I can't prove that your wife cut my vines, but I know she did and so do you. I just want to tell you this right now. If I find one more tree, shrub, or vine on my property that has been meddled with, I will destroy every living thing on your property. You'll not have a single tree or bush left: I guarantee it. I can do it and you'll never be able to prove anything either. So be forewarned. One more act of destruction on your wife's part and that's it.'

"I was sorry to lose a 'friend' permanently, but as the old saw goes, with friends like that, who needs enemies? It's been eighteen months now and nothing more has been touched in my yard since I issued that ultimatum."

Admittedly, this is not the way we would like to solve problems with our neighbors, but sometimes there is no other solution except to threaten retaliation if they keep harassing you, especially when the physical destruction of property is involved.

If you have a neighbor who's kooky or abnormal like this, don't expect normal methods of applied psychology to work. You can't win 'em all!

20

How to Master and Control Large Groups of People

If you have a number of subordinates working under you now, and you're having all sorts of problems directing their activities, this chapter will help you. It will show you the techniques you need to use to master and control large groups of people.

If you are not at the present time in a supervisor's position, let me ask you this: Do you have any idea at all what to do when that time comes? If not, then this chapter will most definitely be of value to you.

Why You Need the Help of Other People

When you want to master and control large groups of people, the first thing you'll find out is that *you cannot possibly direct the actions of each person individually.* The second thing that will come to mind is that *you are going to need help from others to manage and control large numbers of people.* Let me give you a classic example of that.

The Roman Empire stretched from Britain to the Orient. It was the largest unified state the West has ever known. The Romans were noted for developing administrative techniques to control their vast far-flung empire through certain key individuals in strategic government positions.

Theirs was a military empire won by armed conquest. But the same principles of control that were used to govern that empire, namely, *organize*, *deputize*, *supervise*, apply to any large and successful corporation today, be it Xerox, IBM, P&G, whoever.

The chief executive officers of all these giant corporations cannot possibly control their hundreds and thousands of employees all by themselves. They, too, need the help of key executives and able administrators to get the job done. The secret of their success in ruling their industrial or business empires is exactly the same as that of the Roman Emperors—organize, deputize, supervise. Even Genghis Khan, savage barbarian that he was, understood those principles and ruled his vast Asian empire the same way through his loyal tribal chieftains.

When you yourself know how to use these same basic principles of control in your work, there is absolutely no limit as to how high you can go in business or in the number of people you can master and dominate. That's entirely up to you.

OUTSTANDING BENEFITS YOU CAN GAIN

1. *You'll Master and Control Many People Through Just a Few*, when you know how to organize, deputize, and supervise. You see, you don't need to control the whole human race to be successful. You can control dozens of people—yes, even hundreds—through just a few key individuals. The secret of controlling large numbers of people rests solely in your ability to organize, deputize, and supervise.

2. *You Can Save Energy*. The key to saving energy in controlling people is in pinpointing the key person who can help you get the results you want. This is especially useful to those who work with large groups: teachers and preachers; foremen and supervisors; military officers and industrial leaders. But the value of pinpointing the key person isn't limited to those people alone. If you work with as few as half a dozen people—and it doesn't matter whether this is on your job or with your church's finance committee—you can benefit by saving energy and wasted effort, too.

3. *You'll Save Valuable Time*. You'll not only save energy, but you'll also save valuable time when you concentrate your attention on the key individuals who can help you get the job done. And time is important to all of us; we never seem to have enough of it. But the time you spend in finding the specific person who can help you achieve your goals is never wasted.

Take a successful salesman, for instance. Time is his most precious commodity. He will never waste it trying to sell his product to someone who can't make the buying decision. There's an old saying among top-notch salespeople that goes like this: *Sell the secretary on seeing the boss; sell the boss on buying the product.* So my recommendation for saving your valuable time is this: Concentrate your attention on the key individuals who can help you. Don't waste your time and energy on those who can't.

TECHNIQUES YOU CAN USE TO GAIN THESE OUTSTANDING BENEFITS

How You Can Organize, Deputize, and Supervise People for Success

The moment you step into any supervisory position, you learn immediately that you can no longer do everything yourself. Your job as a manager or supervisor is far too big for you to do alone. You are forced to depend on other people whether you like it or not.

If you expect to be successful as a supervisor, you must know how to organize your people and your resources to do the task assigned to you. Next, you must delegate authority to your selected subordinates to do the job. Third, you must supervise to make sure your orders are carried out properly so the work will get done. Let me show you now how to do each one of these.

STEP ONE: HOW TO ORGANIZE YOUR RESOURCES

1. Understand fully the specific job to be done. Know exactly what is required of you.

2. Examine and organize your resources as promptly as possible. Determine the manpower, materials, money, and time that you will need. If certain elements are not available, figure out how you can best improvise.

3. Determine which people you want to assume personal direction of the various phases of the operation. Pick your best personnel, for you'll need to give them full authority to do the job.

As soon as you've decided who your main assistants will be, bring them up-to-date by giving them all the information available.

4. Issue your instructions to those main assistants. Give them enough time to draw up their own plans and issue their orders before setting your project in motion.

5. Give each of your major assistants whatever help he needs to do the job. If you need help from your superior, don't hesitate to ask for it. Just be sure it's necessary when you do.

6. Set a specific time to start and an exact time to complete your project. Once you've made your decision about what to do and how to do it, get on with it. Don't delay.

7. Let your people work without inteference from you. You can use your time for other supervisory responsibilities: inspection, coordination, future planning.

Major Stumbling Blocks

Five major stumbling blocks that keep some supervisors from getting the job done are these:

1. Hesitating to release authority to their assistants so they can do the job.

2. Not giving subordinate leaders enough time to do their own planning.

3. Not asking for additional assistance when it's needed.

4. Being reluctant to initiate action because of the fear of making a mistake.

5. Failing to inspect and supervise the work in progress.

STEP TWO: WHY YOU MUST DEPUTIZE TO GET RESULTS

If you're going to give a person the responsibility for doing a job, you must also give him the authority he needs to carry out that responsibility.

Delegation of authority is not an easy thing to come by. The idea of handing over a job to someone else to do—one that you know perfectly well you can do better yourself—goes against the grain. But, unless you do that, you'll have to do all the work yourself. Then you're not a supervisor, for you're giving up your mastery and control of people, and someone will take your place.

"Many times, I find a supervisor doing the job that a production employee should be doing," says Peggy Hamilton, a department head in a large garment factory. "When I ask that supervisor why she's doing work that rightfully belongs to her subordinate, she says, 'Because it takes me longer to explain how to do it to someone than it takes me to do it myself.'

"Now that may well be true, but it should be true only once. The fallacy of her reasoning is that although it might take her fifteen minutes to explain the job to her subordinate, and only five minutes to do the job herself, she'll have to explain only once if she does it properly.

"When her subordinate has done the job three times, the supervisor has reached the break-even point. From then on she's ahead of the game and can devote her time to something else that she should be doing."

Let me sum up this idea of delegating authority or deputizing someone else to do the job like this. Delegating authority is the point of separation between leaders and followers. If you cannot bring yourself to relinquish the necessary authority to your subordinates to do the job, you are destined to be a follower. You will never be a leader, nor will you be able to master or control anyone. The only way you can possibly master and control large groups of people is to delegate authority to them commensurate with their responsibility. That is the mark of the true leader.

STEP THREE: HOW TO SUPERVISE LIKE A PROFESSIONAL

In Chapter 4 I gave you a brief synopsis to introduce you to the art of supervision. Here I want to expand the scope of this subject so I can help you learn how to supervise and inspect like a real professional.

Supervision is a tool that can make the difference between success and failure. No order is ever complete without the supervisory phase. If all it took were orders to get the job done, you could sit in your easy chair at home and run your entire operation by telephone. But it doesn't work that way at all.

Many times I've been called in to solve a company's labor problems, only to find that the problem was management's failure to supervise. I'm sure you've heard supervisors say, "But it's not my fault; I told him what to do." That age-old excuse from management is lack of supervision; failure to inspect to see that the work is actually being done. Here's a fail-safe procedure you can use to keep that from happening to you.

1. *Set Aside a Part of Your Work Day for Inspections*. Always inspect some phase of your operation every day. Monday mornings and Friday afternoons are the most critical periods of the work week. People tend to slack off during these two times, so bear down on inspections then.

2. *Vary Your Routine*. Don't inspect the same points every Wednesday, the same ones on Friday, that sort of thing. Vary your time schedules, too. People shouldn't be able to set their watches by your inspection routine. Change things around; keep people on their toes.

3. *Review Your Inspection Points Before Inspecting*. Study and review your inspection points *before* you inspect. That way you will never get caught short; your subordinates won't be able to fool you or make you look foolish. You'll always be the expert if you follow this procedure. Don't check any more than eight different points during any one inspection. You can't trust your memory further than that.

4. *Inspect Only Your Selected Points*. You should review your selected points before you inspect so you will know every single thing there is to know about them. Barring an emergency, don't check anything else. Never try to be the expert on everything in one single day. That's absolutely impossible.

5. *To Inspect Is to Emphasize*. Emphasize *your* selected points in your inspection, not the ones your subordinates are trying to select and emphasize for you. Remember who's doing what. You're doing the inspecting; they are being inspected. Not only that, when your subordinate seems anxious to lead you away from the specific point you're interested in, you can be very sure something's wrong with it.

6. *When You Inspect, Bypass the Line of Authority*. This is an absolute must; it is a rigid rule. No other kind of inspection is ever

satisfactory. Your subordinate supervisors can and should go with you on your inspections, but *never question them. Always direct your questions to their subordinates.*

I learned this lesson the hard way when I was in the service as a young platoon officer. Before going on a long hike, I asked the platoon sergeant if every soldier had his raincoat in his pack. The answer was "Yes, sir!" When it started raining on our march, I found out that this was not true. Out of forty-two men, thirty-six had raincoats; six did not.

The next time, I did not ask the sergeant this question. I told him to have each man take his raincoat out of his pack and put it on before we left the company area. It was the only way I could make sure each soldier was properly equipped. That happened nearly forty years ago, and I've been out of the army for a long, long time, but I never forgot the lesson I learned from that one incident.

7. *When You Inspect, Keep Your Ears Open and Listen.* Don't talk except to ask questions. To keep from getting mousetrapped during an inspection, never ask a question to which you don't already know the answer. This is the only way you can find out if your subordinate knows what he is doing.

8. *Recheck the Mistakes You Find.* An inspection is of no value unless you take the necessary action to correct the mistakes you find. So follow up; reinspect. Supervise to make sure your corrective orders are carried out. Remember, always, that *an order without supervision is no order at all.*

Other Benefits That Can Be Gained from Inspections

1. *Inspections Give You Personal Contact with Your People.* It's important for a supervisor to be seen by his subordinates. Even the best worker will get the feeling that the boss doesn't give a continental hoot if he never sees him. So get out from behind your desk. Don't isolate yourself in your office. To see and be seen helps to establish good relationships between a boss and his subordinates.

2. *How to Use Inspections to Improve Relations.* Don't inspect machines; inspect people. Technicians work with things; supervisors work with people. You're a supervisor, not a technician. Use showmanship during your inspections. Make each

inspection a personal visit. Remember first names. Know everything you can about your people; their hobbies, outside interests. Ask about the health of their wives and children. Sincere interest in your subordinates improves morale.

3. *A Subordinate's Performance Can Be Improved by Inspections.* You can use inspections to praise and encourage a person in his work. Performance is always improved by praise, not by criticism. Ask for ideas on how to improve work procedures. This feeds a person's ego and makes him feel more important. Never inspect for the purpose of harassment. Only amateurs do that. Be a professional.

How to Control a Group Through Its Key Persons

The basic rule for controlling a group through its key people is this: *Find out who the key people are in the group and get them on your side first. The rest will automatically follow.*

You see, in every group of people, you will always find certain key individuals who seem to take over naturally. You can spot these key people easily, for they will always be in the center of the action. They do not stand on the sidelines; they are not spectators. They insist on getting into the act. Unlike most people, they really do want to get involved.

It's important to you as a supervisor to identify and recognize these key people in your group, for you'll be able to master and dominate all your subordinates through them. A key personality will usually exhibit the following characteristics:

1. A key person will be an independent and creative thinker.

2. He is an authoritative figure; others turn to him for advice, help, and instructions.

3. A key person always wants to improve the system; he is a natural problem solver.

4. He will have an excellent memory for details, and is knowledgeable in a broad range of subjects.

5. A key person will possess great drive, stamina, and endurance.

So, no matter how many persons you work with or how many are in the group you want to influence and control, it's essential that you locate these key people before you try to do anything else. You'll get results when you do. Knowing who the key people are is a must when you need action and you need it right now. They can get that action for you when and where you most need it.

Taking Command of a Group Requires Courage

If you show the slightest hesitancy or exhibit the least bit of fear, you will never succeed in maintaining control of a group of people, be that group your subordinates at work, the PTA, a church group, a social committee, or whatever.

Just remember this. When you give orders, people will automatically assume that you have the right to do so. Even more important, they will also assume that you know what you're doing. It's all a question of style and courage. Simply put, controlling a group of people takes good old-fashioned guts.

The Secret of
Verbal Brainwashing

Because of the Nazis and the Communists, "brainwashing" has become an ugly word to some people. But the purpose of those two extremist groups was to purge a person's mind of his political, economic, and social ideas and attitudes so that he would become completely willing to accept their views. Severe and inhumane physical and psychological measures were used to frighten, confuse, bewilder, degrade, mistreat, even torture their subjects so they could gain their objectives. The means did not matter to them; it was only the end result that counted.

But you and I are not at all interested in this kind of brainwashing. Your purpose should be to offer an individual certain benefits that he wants to gain and that he can get when he does as you desire. It is certainly not illegal or immoral for you to use brainwashing as a powerful but fully legitimate technique of persuasion to convert a person to your way of thinking so he will do what you want him to do. That's really the method that is used all the time by sharp advertisers, for example, to convince a person using product A to stop and switch over the product B. That's the way they use brainwashing as a legal and thoroughly legitimate sales technique.

You can do the same; that is, you can convince a person that it is best for him to do what you want him to do by plugging all the benefits he'll gain when he does. In fact, brainwashing is most successful when your subject reaches the point where he really *wants* to do what you desire. When he reaches that point in his thinking, you've truly gained complete mastery over him.

HOW YOU CAN USE BRAINWASHING FOR YOUR OWN BENEFIT

1. *You'll Gain a Personal Power and Mastery over Others,* greater than anything you've ever experienced before when you use the brainwashing techniques I'll give you in this chapter. Prestige, status, respect, influence—all these can be yours. People will have to yield to you and provide you with whatever you want.

2. *Brainwashing Will Make You a Real Leader of Others.* You'll not be just a persuader or a manipulator of people, but a true leader of others. Virtually everything that you demand, people will now have to give you.

3. *Your Personal Magnetism and Charisma Will Grow Stronger and Stronger,* when you know how to use verbal brainwashing. People will not only agree with you, but they will also be anxious to do whatever you want or help you get whatever you desire.

4. *Your Personal Power Will Literally Become Self-Generating.* It will start multiplying and growing all of its own accord. People will be drawn to you as if by a magnet to offer you business deals, social honors, positions of leadership and respect. Even the big job or executive position that you've always wanted for yourself can now be yours.

5. *Your Knowledge of How to Gain Complete Mastery over Others Will Almost Be Complete,* when you add brainwashing to your arsenal of techniques. When you look in the mirror now, you'll see a completely changed, confident and positive-minded individual; one who commands new talents, power, influence and respect. You can now get everything you want out of life; every single thing you've ever desired can now be yours.

TECHNIQUES YOU CAN USE TO GAIN THESE MARVELOUS BENEFITS

What Verbal Brainwashing Actually Is and How It Works

To completely remove any misunderstanding you could still have about brainwashing and to eliminate any apprehension you might feel about using it as a technique to gain mastery over people, let me explain to you exactly what it is and precisely how it works.

First of all, it is important to know that your mind is divided into two major parts: *the conscious mind and the subconscious mind.* Each of these has its own separate and distinct function.

Your Conscious Mind Thinks. It uses logic and reason, intellect and intelligence, past experience and learning, to reach its conclusions and make its decisions.

Your Subconscious Mind Feels. It is the source of intuition, imagination, and inspiration. If your conscious mind tells you something is right by logic and reason, but an inner hunch causes you to feel something is wrong, that inner hunch is coming from your subconscious mind. Listen to it well, for your subconscious mind is the storehouse of memory. Although your conscious mind may have forgotten some long-ago incident, it will never be erased from your subconscious mind.

How You Can Brainwash Someone Else's Subconscious Mind

An important point to remember about the subconscious mind is that it accepts suggestions and takes orders, not only from its own conscious mind, *but also from outside sources when its own conscious mind is bypassed.* Let me show you now by an example how this works.

Let's suppose you're on a luxurious Caribbean cruise. You approach a fearful-looking passenger and say something like this: "You look very ill. Your face is terribly pale. You must be getting seasick. If you'd like, I'll help you to your cabin."

This person, who has been afraid all the time about getting seasick, now becomes extremely ill, all as a result of the simple suggestion you planted in his subconscious mind. He is much like Job who said, "For the thing which I greatly feared is come upon me."

But if you were to make that same suggestion to a seasoned seagoing traveler or a sailor, he would probably laugh at you. After many voyages, he knows he has nothing to worry about. Therefore, his conscious mind rejects your suggestion and does not allow it to enter his subconscious mind.

As you progress in your knowledge, understanding, and actual practice of using verbal brainwashing to gain mastery over people, you will find that some persons are much more susceptible to outside suggestions and orders than others. It's entirely up to you to find out who they are.

Another Highly Effective Brainwashing Technique You Can Use

Another significant point to remember about brainwashing is that *fatigue increases the subconscious mind's susceptibility to suggestions or orders from sources outside its own conscious mind.*

You see, normally a person's conscious mind acts like a guard at the gate. It filters out unwanted information and keeps it from entering the storehouse of memory in the subconscious mind.

But when a person is tired and worn out, the conscious mind drops its watchful guard. It fails to fulfill its function of protecting the subconscious mind from outside suggestions and influences. Here's how this information can be useful to you.

Let's say, for example, that you want your husband to do a certain thing for you, but you want to plant the thought so subtly in his subconscious mind that he'll think the whole idea was his very own. To do that, whisper your message softly in his ear several times when he's relaxing in his easy chair in front of the TV after a hard day at the office and a big satisfying meal. If your husband stirs and asks you what you said, just answer, "Oh, nothing, dear. I'm sorry I disturbed you." You can also whisper the same idea in his ear after he's gone to bed just after he drops off to sleep. Don't worry; his subconscious mind will hear you. It never sleeps.

These are the two perfect times to practice this technique, for both fatigue and physical inertia favor mental relaxation and passivity, thus making your husband's subconscious mind more receptive to suggestion. It may take you several weeks or even months to get results, but don't worry, you'll get what you want if you don't give up. Constant implantation in his subconscious mind by repetition of what you desire is the key to your eventual success.

My wife tells me that a friend of hers wanted to get her husband to take her to the fabulous Mexican resort city of Acapulco for their annual vacation, so she used this method on him night after night. She was about ready to give up, when one day he came home with a handful of travel folders on Mexico, and said, "Let's go to Acapulco this summer on our vacation, shall we?"

What about going after a raise from your boss or asking him for a special favor that you want? Catch him in the late afternoon when he's tired and worn out and relaxing for a few moments. He'll be more susceptible to your suggestion than he will be in the morning when he's bright-eyed, fresh, and alert.

Better yet, nail him for what you want when he has a cold or is coming down with the flu. Sure, he might be grouchy, but he's still more vulnerable at that time. Illness is even more effective than fatigue as an intensifier of suggestibility.

Why the Most Effective Advertising Is a Form of Brainwashing

Commercial sponsors of television advertising prefer the evening hours for plugging their products. If you were to ask them why, they would say that there are more television viewers in the evening.

Although this is true, it is not the only reason for their preference for advertising in the evening hours. Another major reason is that people are tired and worn out in the evening and fatigue increases the subconscious mind's susceptibility to suggestions from outside sources.

Also, physical inertia favors mental relaxation and passivity, thus making the subconscious mind more receptive to external suggestions. Since most of us spend our evening hours relaxing in a soft easy chair in front of the TV set, we are all perfect targets for the astute advertiser.

As one authority in the advertising business said, "During the day, a person's willpower resists with the greatest possible energy any attempt at being forced to succumb to another person's will. In the evening, however, when a person is fatigued, he will give in much more easily to suggestions from an outside source. That's why sponsors are perfectly willing to pay a higher price for nighttime television commercials."

An executive with a nationwide soft drink company told me this: "We don't really care if a person doesn't remember what we say about our product. All we ask is that he remember the *name* of our soft drink so he'll ask for it automatically without even thinking when he goes to the grocery store."

That's exactly the response you want from your subject. You want him to automatically do what you want without even thinking about it. If brainwashing will do that for advertisers of commercial products, and we know that it will, it'll work for you, too.

How You Can Use Brainwashing to Change Behavior Patterns

Let me first give you a classic example of how to use brainwashing to change behavior patterns. Then you can adopt your own version and develop your own procedures to fit your specific needs.

John Wesley, the founder of the Methodist faith, enjoyed an enormous success as an English evangelist. He had a shrewd and intuitive understanding of the inner workings of the human mind.

He would open his sermon with a long and vivid description of the agonies and torture to which his listeners would be condemned for all eternity unless they became converted to the faith. Then, after a sense of terror, guilt, and extreme anxiety had brought his audience to the brink of a complete nervous breakdown, he would offer eternal salvation to those who accepted Christ and repented of their sins.

By this kind of preaching, Wesley converted hundreds and thousands of people. Intense prolonged fear exhausted their nervous systems and produced a state of greatly intensified suggestibility in their subconscious minds. In this vulnerable condition, people accepted the preacher's theological message without question. They emerged from this religious ordeal with new behavior patterns firmly planted in their subconscious minds.

You may not want to use such drastic measures to change the behavior patterns of your spouse or your children, but you can develop some effective techniques of your own. The important point to remember is that if new behavior patterns are implanted in the subconscious mind when the conscious mind is exhausted, brainwashing will always work. Given the right circumstances and appropriate conditions, you can convert anybody to anything.

Let me give you an example of how you can make this procedure work for you. Thelma's husband, Stanley, was a chain cigarette smoker of three to four packs a day. Thelma was greatly concerned for his health. Each night as he sat in his easy chair in front of the TV half asleep, and, again, after he had gone to bed, she would whisper softly in his ear several times, "Cigarettes cause lung cancer; stop smoking!"

Several months passed and Thelma was about ready to give up when one day Stanley said to her, "I've decided to quit smoking." When she asked why, he replied, "I don't really know why. It's just that something inside me keeps telling me not to smoke any more, so I'm not going to." That was more than six years ago; Stanley hasn't smoked a single cigarette since then.

How to Brainwash Yourself for Total Success in Whatever You Do

You can learn to program your subconscious mind for total success in whatever you do if you use certain techniques that I'll show you. But first, let me give you an example of how it works.

Suppose you have a problem that you simply cannot find the answer to. Your conscious mind works at it until it is exhausted, but still the solution fails to come. Finally in despair you let it go and dismiss it from your conscious mind when you go to bed. The next morning when your conscious mind starts to think about your problem again, the answer suddenly appears, seemingly from nowhere. What happened? Your subconscious mind solved the problem for you while you were sound asleep.

A friend of mine, also an author, told me this: "Very often I have awakened in the morning to find a problem of technique, or plot, or character, which had been troubling me when I went to bed, completely solved while I've been asleep."

If you've never used this procedure, try it. Consciously turn your unsolved problem over to your subconscious mind when you go to bed at night. You'll be astounded at the results you can get when you let your subconscious mind take over.

You can also program your subconscious mind for total success in the daytime. Scott C. was an average salesman until he learned how to use his subconscious mind. Each morning as he stood in front of his bathroom mirror, he would say to his reflection, "You are an outstanding success. You are making fifty thousand dollars a year."

He also had photos taken of himself sitting in a Lincoln Continental and standing in front of a magnificent colonial-style mansion. He taped these pictures to his bathroom mirror. He also made a cassette tape recording that told him how successful he was, how much money he was making, what his specific goals were. He played this tape night after night after going to bed just before dropping off to sleep when his subconscious mind was fully receptive to autosuggestion. The end result of all this effort? Before the year was out, Scott's salary and commissions far exceeded his $50,000 goal, he had the new Lincoln, and had made the down payment on the house of his dreams.

The subconscious mind accepts not only what you say to it, but also information that is presented to it in pictures. It takes whatever you give it as the truth and as having already taken place. The subconscious mind works on the principle of *believe that you have it and you shall have it.*

You can also use pictures to rid yourself of undesirable habits. Fran C. took photographs of herself when she weighed nearly 200 pounds. She taped one on the refrigerator door, another on the pantry door, and still another on her bathroom scale. Beside each fat picture of herself, she placed a photo taken when she weighed only 115 pounds. For the first time, she succeeded in losing weight permanently when she'd failed every time before on diet plans. Why did she succeed this time? Because she gave her subconscious mind the information it needed to go to work for her.

Raymond O. had a drinking problem. His wife took a picture of him after he'd passed out in a big easy chair after a party. Someone had placed a lampshade on his head for a hat, his shirt was torn and half off, and his trousers had been unzipped and were open. She put this picture on the door of his liquor cabinet. Beside it she put the picture of him that was taken on his wedding day. When Ray saw the photos, he became so disgusted with himself, that he never drank again. He changed because in his subconscious mind he simply could no longer accept himself as a drunk.

You, too, can program your subconscious mind by using pictures. In many cases, the subconscious mind will accept pictures even better than words. If you want to be successful in some endeavor, don't just say it with words alone. Picture yourself as being completely successful to better impress your subconscious mind.

Why Repetition Is the Key to Success in Brainwashing

Do not expect the subconscious mind to change a person's habits or behavior patterns if a new idea is planted in it only once. The subconscious mind does not work that way. Constant repetition is the key to success in brainwashing. For instance, it takes the average person at least 38 repetitions to commit a simple thing to memory. If the material to be memorized is complicated, like Lincoln's Gettysburg Address, for example, more than 400 repetitions are required by the average person to implant the information permanently in the subconscious mind's storehouse of memory.

So, if you want to change your own or someone else's habits and behavior patterns, be patient and remember that repetition is the key to success. Just as dripping water wears away a rock, so will repetition of the same idea wear down a person's resistance.

To sum up this chapter briefly, let me say that if you use brainwashing on a person when he is mentally and physically exhausted, when he is relaxed and his conscious mind's guard is down, or when he is sick, it will always work. Under favorable conditions, practically anyone can be converted to almost anything. Brainwashing is a sure way to gain power and mastery over people.

Now let's get on to the next chapter and another subject that is just as exciting and interesting: "How to Get People to Tell You Their Secrets."

22

How to Get People to Tell You Their Secrets

For our purposes here, we are not interested in such secrets as neighborhood gossip about what marriage is about to break up; who's sleeping with whom; who has a drinking problem; why Mrs. Brown isn't speaking to Mrs. Jones, that sort of thing. Secrets like that are of no value whatever to you in gaining power and mastery over people. We're interested in learning the secrets of successful and popular people so we can use that information to our best advantage.

TREMENDOUS BENEFITS YOU'LL GAIN

Let me give you a few examples of the tremendous benefits you can gain from this chapter. For instance...

1. *You Can Improve Your Own Sales Performance* when you learn the techniques that super salespeople use to get to the top. If you're not in sales work, that's all right, too. You can use the same techniques in your church or social activities to take charge. You can use them on your spouse to get him or her to see things your way and to do what you want.

2. *You Can Get Your Own Way Every Time* when you learn the secret of prying information out of a person for your own benefit. This is a technique you can use to great advantage on tough bosses, obstinate customers and clients, stubborn authorities, and anyone else who's been holding you back from big money and success.

3. *You'll Learn the Secret of Popularity*. This technique will automatically allow you to feel right at home and act correctly in any social environment. You can walk into any group and be as much at ease as if you were with your own family. Others will be anxious to talk to you, to be with you, to gain your friendship.

4. *You'll Learn How to Guard Your Business Secrets* when you follow the guidelines I'll give you in the last technique. This is highly important to you, for the spy in the corporate structure is not a myth. He's real. And if he's a she instead, you must be doubly careful if you're a man. She can clip you as easily as Delilah sheared Samson.

TECHNIQUES YOU CAN USE TO GAIN THESE BENEFITS

How to Get a Person to Tell You His Secret Without Even Asking Him

You can use one of several methods to get a person to tell you his secrets without even asking him to do so. For instance...

1. *A Secret Makes a Person Feel Superior to You Because He Knows Something That You Don't*. Maybe it's something the boss told him about some future plan or some operation that's going to take place later on. Whatever it is, let him enjoy his moment of glory. Make him feel even more important. Feed his ego by saying that the boss doesn't tell everybody these things; only the people he trusts. Then drop the subject as if you're no longer interested. He'll immediately want to tell you what it's all about, for only by doing so can he really let you know how important he is. The more important the secret, the more important he will feel, but only when he tells you. After all, a secret is no fun alone; it has to be shared with someone to be enjoyed to its fullest.

2. *Acting As if the Secret Is Already Common Knowledge* is another method you can use to get a secret out of a person. Just say, "Oh yes, I know about that. The boss told me that yesterday." When he wants to know what the boss told you, slough him off by saying, "Oh, that's confidential, and I really couldn't tell *you*." His normal reaction to this is to tell you what the secret is *so he can prove he's really on the inside, too*. Now you both know.

3. *Ask the Right Kind of Questions* and you can usually learn the secret about anything. One way of doing this is simply to say, "This is what I think, but, of course, my viewpoint may be different from yours. What's your own idea on this?" This is usually enough to get the other person talking, and sooner or later the secret will surface without your even asking for it.

To summarize this idea, just remember that people want to tell you their secrets so you'll know just how important they really are. I've yet to meet the person who isn't anxious to have the secret "pried" out of him. If he didn't want you to know his secret, he wouldn't have mentioned it to you in the first place. Humor him, baby him, nurse him along, and before it's over, he'll tell you everthing you want to know.

Secrets of Super Salespeople

I've revealed several secrets to you already in previous chapters that top salespeople use to gain mastery over others. Here's one that most super salesmen and women place right at the top of the list.

Jessica M., a highly successful mutual fund saleswoman in a business that's usually regarded as strictly a man's world, says that it's highly important to get your prospect to say *yes* immediately.

"I word all my questions to a new prospect so the only possible answer is *yes*," Jessica says. "For instance, I say, 'Would you like to have your investment risk reduced to an absolute minimum?' Of course the answer always has to be *yes*. I might follow up this question with 'If I can show you how you can gain the maximum return on your investment along with that minimum risk, would you be interested?' Again, the answer has to be *yes*.

"You can use many other ways to phrase questions to insure a yes answer. The important thing is getting the prospect to say *yes* so continuously that when the final buying decision has to be made, the word *yes* just falls out of his mouth automatically."

You can use the same procedure on your wife, your husband, your children, your friends and associates, whoever. Just get the other person to say *yes* at the beginning. Keep him from saying *no* by the way you word your questions.

A "yes" answer not only establishes the right psychological frame of mind, but also the correct *physiological* condition in his body. All the processes of the body are in an accepting, relaxed, and open attitude.

By the same token, a single "no" changes all these psychological and physiological processes into a fighting, defiant mood of rejection. All the body systems—glandular, muscular, neurological—prepare themselves for combat. If your wife or husband, your children, a prospective customer and client, or your boss says "No!" to you at the very beginning, it almost requires a miracle to change that person's negative response to a positive one.

Plan your approach so you can get an affirmative answer from the person at the very start. If you want to win people over to your way of thinking, if you want to make a sale or make a friend, then get the other person to say "yes" to you immediately. You'll get your own way every single time when you do. This technique is a secret of super salespeople. Use it; it will give you unlimited mastery over people, and that's the name of the game.

The Secret of Prying Information Out of a Person for Your Benefit

In previous chapters I've told you that people will usually have two reasons for doing or not doing something: one reason that sounds good to the listener and another that he keeps hidden all to himself.

At that time I also mentioned that one of the best ways to drag that hidden reason out of a person was to keep on asking, "And in addition to that?" or "Isn't there some other reason you object to this?" This method of questioning is extremely valuable when you're trying to change a reluctant prospect into a solid customer.

But there are other methods you can use when you want to get information, not only out of a prospective client or customer, but also out of other people such as the members of your family or your employees. The most powerful word in the English language you can use to keep the other person talking so you can learn what you want to know is a simple little three-letter one, "why." Let me give you an example so you can see for yourself how well this works:

A friend of mine, Arthur Dunlap, for years used to say that he didn't believe in life insurance. So I was really surprised the other day when he told me he'd bought a $100,000 policy from a young fellow the week before. When I asked him how in the world this had happened, here's what he told me:

"When this young man came calling on me, I told him I didn't believe in life insurance. Instead of arguing with me as all the other salesmen had done before, he simply asked, 'Why?'

"Well, I explained to him why, but every time I stopped for breath, he'd ask, 'Why?,' and the more I talked, the more I realized there was something the matter with my argument. Finally, I convinced myself that I was wrong, so I bought some insurance.

"That young man didn't sell me anything. He just kept asking me 'Why?' I made the sale and he made the profit! Smartest salesman I've ever met."

I covered this subject of how to use "why?" in a seminar I gave for salesmen in Orlando, Florida. A few weeks later, I received a letter from one of the young men who'd attended the course. The gist of it went like this:

"I'd been trying for more than a year to sell our latest computerized diagnostic equipment to a large automobile service center here, but I hadn't been successful.

"So this time when I went to call on the owner and he said he wasn't interested, I asked him *why.*

"'Because your equipment is too expensive,' he said. 'It would never pay for itself.'

"'Why?' I asked him.

"He looked surprised at my question, for I'd never asked him that before. 'Do you think it would?' he asked.

"'Why not?' I said. 'Everyone who's bought it so far thinks it's a terrific investment. It's brought in a lot more business for all of them.'

"Well, we kept seesawing back and forth like that for an hour. Each time he offered an objection, I countered with *why* or *why not.* Finally, he saw that all his objections just didn't add up, so he ordered the equipment.

"I can't get over how easy that sale was to make. Actually, he sold himself where I hadn't been able to do so for more than a year. My commission on that one sale paid for the expenses of your seminar several times over."

As I've said, you don't need to be in business or in the sales profession to use this highly effective *why* technique. You can use it in church, PTA, your club, or in any social activity you can think of to get your own way. It will always work.

Use this *why* technique yourself the next time you want someone to do something and he's hesitant at first. He'll actually end up convincing himself that what you're asking is the right thing for him to do. It's one of the easiest ways I know of to gain mastery over people.

How I Learned the Secret of Wayne's Popularity

Wayne V. is one of the most popular persons I've ever met. He's always being invited somewhere. Someone is constantly after him to go to a party, have lunch at the club, be the guest speaker at the Rotary or the Kiwanis, play golf or tennis.

One evening, I happened to be a guest at a small social gathering at a friend's home. I spotted Wayne sitting in a corner with the prettiest girl there. Out of curiosity I watched for a while from a distance. I noticed that the young lady was talking constantly, but Wayne never seemed to say a word. He would smile and nod his head every so often and that was it. After a couple of hours, they got up, thanked their host and hostess, and left.

The next day, I saw Wayne in a restaurant eating lunch alone for a change so I asked if I could join him. "I saw you with the most gorgeous girl at the Swansons' last night," I said. "She seemed to be totally engrossed in you. How did you hold her attention so well?"

"Easy," Wayne said. "When Mrs. Swanson introduced Jo Ann to me, I simply said to her, 'You have a gorgeous tan. And right in the middle of winter, too, How did you do it? Where have you been? Acapulco? Hawaii?'

"'Hawaii,' she told me. 'It was ever so wonderful.'

"'Would you tell me all about it?' I said.

"'I'd love to,' she replied. So we sat down in a quiet corner and for the next two hours she did just exactly that.

"This morning Jo Ann called me to say she'd enjoyed my company very much. She said she was eager to see me again, for I was a most interesting person to talk with. But to tell the truth, I didn't say more than a dozen words all night long."

Have you figured out Wayne's secret of popularity yet? It's ever so simple. All Wayne did was get Jo Ann to talk about herself.

He uses the same technique on everyone. He says to a person, "Please tell me all about it." That's all it takes to turn the average individual on for a couple of hours. People love Wayne for the way he pays attention to them.

If you, too, want to be popular with everyone, never, never talk about yourself. Instead, get the other person talking about *his* interests, *his* business, *his* golf scores, *his* successes, *her* children, *her* hobbies, *her* trip, and so on.

Just get people to talk about themselves, listen with undivided attention, and you'll be popular, too. You'll be welcome wherever you go. Here are some techniques you can use to keep a person talking about himself.

1. *Look at the Person While He's Talking.* Don't be disturbed by anything else. The person will notice that immediately and be upset by your lack of attention.

2. *Show Interest in What He Is Saying.* You don't need to say a word. Just nod your head and smile when it's called for. That's all you need do.

3. *Lean Toward the Person.* This evidences a deep interest on your part in what the person is saying.

4. *Ask Questions if Necessary.* All you need do is say something like, "And then what did you do?" "And then what did you say?" That's enough to keep the person going indefinitely.

5. *Don't Interrupt.* A person doesn't like to be interrupted. Have you ever been in the middle of a good story only to have someone interrupt and change the subject completely? You'd like to have strangled him, right? The person to whom you're listening feels exactly the same way if you interrupt him.

How to Keep Your Secrets to Yourself

In discussing how to get people to tell you their secrets, I would be remiss if I did not tell you the measures you can use to keep people from learning your secrets. I'm referring especially to those individuals who could prevent you from reaching your goals if they learn about your business plans or intentions.

Whether you're in business for yourself or working for a big company, you can use the following checklist to keep your business secrets safe and secure.

1. *Consider All Company Business as Confidential.* To keep your competitor from learning your trade secrets, your business plans, and your future projects, consider all company business as confidential. Just because a person's on your payroll, don't assume that he's automatically loyal to you. He could have been planted by your competition. It happens.

2. *Don't Discuss Business Outside the Office.* Never discuss *confidential* matters outside the office. If you're not sure what's confidential and what's not, consider it all classified. The best rule is to keep *business* business in the office and *personal* business at home. That way you'll never go wrong.

3. *Never Brag About Your Business Successes.* It's fine to tell *what* your company did, but keep the *how* locked up in your head. The trouble is, when you brag about success, it just naturally leads to methods and procedures, for your listener always wants to know how you did it. But the how is your business, not his. One of the best ways to brag is to smile all the way to the bank.

4. *Guard Your Company Secrets as You Would Your Daughter's Morals.* The formula for Coca-Cola has been a closely guarded secret for decades and it still is; so is the secret recipe for Colonel Sanders' Kentucky Fried Chicken. If you want to keep ahead of your competition, don't give away your trade secrets. If they've made you successful, keep them secret so you can continue to be successful.

5. *Don't Tell Employment Agencies All the Job Specifics.* If you use the services of an employment agency, it's enough to say that you're looking for a chemical engineer with a degree and five or six years' experience. That's all you need say. The person you hire can learn the job specifics after he goes to work.

6. *Don't Leave Confidential Notes or Documents on Your Desk.* If you leave your desk for coffee or lunch, put the secret notes and papers in your desk and lock it. The average subordinate cannot resist taking a quick peek at papers on your desk, especially if they're hidden away in a folder marked "Confidential." That word is like a green light to him.

7. *Lock All Desks and File Cabinets at Night.* I know this can be a nuisance until you get used to it. But to make any system work,

you must work the system. Quit five minutes early and use that time to clean up your area.

8. *Destroy All Waste Paper Daily; Especially Carbon Paper.* This, too, can be a nuisance if you allow it to become one. But, if you want to guard your secrets, it's a must. An incinerator is a good investment. If you can't use one because of local clean air regulations, consider purchasing a paper shredder.

9. *Operate on a Need-to-Know Basis.* Let a person know only what he needs to know to do his job, nothing more. It's the best way to protect your own interests and guard your business secrets.

23

How to Be an Influential Member or Effective Leader of Any Club, Organization, or Community

First of all, let me say that the techniques I'll give you here can be used to gain power in any organization or community, be that organization a church, a social club, a fraternal lodge, a civic association, or that community a large city, a county, a small town, a village, a subdivision, or a neighborhood. You can use these techniques to gain mastery over people anywhere; that's the sole purpose of this chapter.

Wherever you are, you'll always find that certain people have taken the reins of leadership into their own hands. You'll soon find that it isn't necessarily *what* you know, but *whom* you know that counts in getting ahead.

For example, in the small Iowa town of 2,000 in which I grew up, the church a person belonged to was the vital factor in determining social status, position, and power. Most farmers belonged to the Christian church. Merchants, shopkeepers, and business people, as well as their employees, were Methodists. The powerful and influential people of the town—doctors, lawyers, bankers, newspaper publishers—went to the Presbyterian church. How important was this in this small Iowa town? Let me give you an example to illustrate this point.

A certain prosperous farmer was a member of the Christian church. He ran for county sheriff on two occasions, and although he was well liked by most people, he was defeated. He then moved to town and joined the Presbyterian church. Shortly thereafter, he ran for sheriff again and this time he was elected. He was elected time and again to serve nearly twenty years in that position. You see, as soon as he became a member of that inner circle of power— although a minor one at first—he succeeded in gaining what he wanted.

BENEFITS YOU CAN GAIN WHEN YOU JOIN THAT INNER CIRCLE OF POWER

1. *You'll Gain Personal Power and Mastery over Others.* You too, just like the sheriff I told you about, can gain mastery over others when you join that inner circle of power. You can become the leader in all the social, family, business, and political, community, and neighborhood matters in which you participate. You can be elected to the presidency and chairmanship of clubs, groups, and associations. Wherever you go, you'll be known as a powerful and influential person. Power and mastery over others will be yours.

2. *Financial Reward Is a Dividend of Membership in That Inner Circle of Power.* People will come to you to offer you business deals, social honors, positions of financial leadership and respect, perhaps even the big job or high-paying position you've always wanted. Your great power over others and your mastery of them will make them provide you with whatever you want in life.

POWER TECHNIQUES YOU CAN USE TO GAIN THESE MAGNIFICENT BENEFITS

How to Spot the "Inner Circle" of Power

You don't have to be a detective to spot the inner circle of power. For instance, most smaller communities have roads, streets, and parks named after a prominent citizen. In that small town I grew up in, we had a Hamilton street and a Hamilton drive, both named after a wealthy and influential county judge. Our city park was Bonebright Park, named after the publisher of the county's leading weekly newspaper. The same situation exists where I live today in Florida, except that various parks, streets, and roads are named after the senior member of the county commission.

City council members, county commission members, and other local politicians, especially those who determine where and how our tax dollars are spent, enjoy immense power and prestige.

You can also spot leaders in the community if you join the local chamber of commerce. You don't have to attend many meetings to find out who dictates policy. Certain names will constantly be heard. You'll often hear remarks like, "Better check with Sam before we do this; he might have a different idea," or "Joe told me before the meeting what his feelings were; I think we'd better go along with him on this."

Sometimes that power can be found in a commercial organization. One particular land and home development corporation in the southwestern United States is and has been for many years the power in the community. When the president of the company speaks, the police chief and the mayor hop to carry out his orders.

The organization built a private country club and golf course right in the middle of their residential area. Residents are automatically entitled to club membership, although they must pay for that privilege. But complimentary memberships are offered to prominent citizens outside the community who support the company's plans, policies, and procedures. This irritates the residents, but as long as the organization retains its power base and controls the purse strings in the community, the practice will continue.

How to Become a Member of That "Inner Power Circle"

As soon as you find out where that "inner power circle" is, join that group, be it the chamber of commerce, a country club, a lodge such as the Masons, the Eagles, Elks, Moose, or an organization such as the Kiwanis or the Rotary Club.

If you're a staunch member of some particular religious denomination, I'm not going to tell you to change churches, as the farmer who became sheriff did, but if you believe that all roads lead to heaven, then I'd recommend that, too. One of today's most prominent television evangelists changed denominations when it was advantageous for him to do so.

When you do become a member of the organization that contains the inner power circle, don't be a passive one. You'll get absolutely nowhere that way. As professional musicians put it, "You have to pay your dues with one-night stands, scruffy clubs, and low pay before you can expect to become an 'overnight success.'"

So you must be prepared to pay your dues, too, by being an active member of the organization you joined. It's the only way you can make your name known where it counts. Don't hesitate or refuse to serve on any committee. Don't be bashful or afraid to join in any of the club's activities.

Some members of an organization get the idea that if they pay their financial dues, or do some litle bit of service, they have performed their full duty. These people are not leaders at all; they are only followers, and their names will soon be forgotten. A person who is accepted into a community organization of some sort is taken in for the service he can contribute, not for the membership fees he pays.

Active service in the organization makes you an important member of your community. This builds up your reputation and helps make your name a household word. Then, when a member of that inner circle of power wants something done, he'll ask for you as automatically as a person who wants a soft drink asks for a Coke.

Making Your Approach to the Power Broker

Don't wait for the power broker to come to you. It's not going to happen. It's up to you to go to him first and offer your services. Let him know you're available. You can find any number of ways to do favors for the top individuals in the organization, not in an obsequious and servile manner, but as one equal to another.

What can you offer him? Go right back to the basics; your list of the learned needs and desires that every person has. You can't help but find at least one desire you can fulfill for that person of power. He might have everything in life that he wants or needs, but there's one desire he has that he can never get enough of: *the desire for a feeling of importance.* Let me give you an example.

Paul J. Meyer, the founder and president of the multimillion dollar corporation, SMI International, Inc., the country's leading producer of managerial, motivational, and leadership cassette tapes which are distributed worldwide, got his start selling insurance in Florida.

The inspiration that eventually led to the founding of SMI came to Mr. Meyer at a yacht basin in Jacksonville. Mr. Meyer reasoned that anyone who had a yacht must also have some good ideas on how to become rich and successful. He jotted down the license numbers of those yacht club Lincolns and Cadillacs, traced the owners, and then asked them, sincerely and honestly, to what they attributed their financial success.

These people were so impressed by Mr. Meyer's sincere approach that they answered his questions without hesitation. You see, *in spite of all their money, these wealthy people still craved attention and wanted to feel important*. It's hard for you and me to understand, perhaps, but it's still true. These rich people had Cadillacs, Lincolns, yachts, mansions, and everything else that money could buy. *But they still craved attention. They still needed ego gratification*.

Mr. Meyer gave them what they wanted: *a feeling of importance*. In return, they gave him what he wanted, *information*. He took their answers, sifted them, expanded them, and reassembled them along with some original concepts of his own. The end result was called a "Blueprint for Success." It became the foundation for SMI's first course.

Mr. Meyer gained mastery over people by making them feel important. You can do the same in approaching the power broker. Make him feel even more important than he already is. You'll never go wrong when you do.

How to Find the Real Power Behind the Throne

At times, the real power is hidden and the person sitting on the throne is only a figurehead. If that's the case, it's up to you to find out who's really pulling the power strings. You must know who it is, for you need him on your side if you expect to become successful.

Even in church organizations, the power doesn't always lie exclusively with the elders and the deacons. Sometimes it can be found in the most unexpected places. Let me give you an example:

"I am always willing that the church should raise my salary," says Stewart Clark, pastor of a large Missouri church with a 2,500-member congregation and an hour of television coverage on Sunday mornings. "Over the years I've found that the church that pays the largest salary always raises it the easiest. Based on that, I suppose I needn't worry about it right now. Still, it's something I've learned never to take for granted.

"When the time comes for my church to consider a salary increase for me, I concentrate my attention on the budget and finance committee to show them how easily we can afford my raise. I personally don't try to sell my whole congregation on the idea. I let the committee do that for me.

"However, I've learned something else, too, through the years. Not all of the key people are on the budget and finance committee. Power and influence can be found in the most unexpected places at times. So I always keep my eyes on that little old lady who says, 'I really don't know why the girls always ask me for advice and help, honestly I don't. After all, I'm not on any of the church's official committees. Of course, I'm always willing to do what I can to help out. In fact, when we're holding a church supper or having a bazaar to raise money, they always call me to ask what I want them to do!'

"So I watch out for her, my friend. She's the one I'll need on my side to get my increase in salary. She's the real power behind the throne." (As you've probably already guessed by now, Stewart Clark is not the pastor's real name. I wouldn't want that little old lady to keep him from getting his next pay raise!)

How to Be Your PR Agent

Not only do you need to be a member of the "right" organization, but you'll also need to let people know just how good you really are. So plan on becoming your own public relations agent. If you're going to become a household name in the community, you need to become well known. People must recognize your name immediately.

To do that, get your name in the newspaper whenever possible. Offer to speak to church or civic groups without any sort of reimbursement as long as they promise to send notices to local papers to publicize the event.

If you are an authority on any subject, get on local radio and television talk shows. Program directors develop ulcers trying to find the right people and get enough material to fill their local programming requirements. They'll welcome you with open arms if your subject is timely and interesting and if you really know what you're talking about.

Do everything you can to make your name known. When you

go to church, don't sit in the back pews. Go up front where everybody can see you. Sing with gusto and enthusiasm (that is, if you sing on key!) so that people will notice you. And if you go to Sunday School as well as to the preaching service, enter into the discussion with verve and vigor. As a friend of mine, Bill Reiners, says, "I may not be an authority on the subject you're talking about, but I'll have an opinion on it, you can bet on that!"

To sum up this idea of how to be your own press agent or your own public relations man, let me say this: If you don't blow your own horn, no one else will, so toot away and enjoy it.

Personal Qualifications You Need for Leadership

I could list a dozen or more qualities you should have for community leadership; for instance, you should excel in teamwork, you should be a good teacher, you must be courageous, possess initiative, and be adept at overcoming difficulties, just to mention a few.

However, because of time and space limitations, I have selected five major qualities for community leadership that I'd like to discuss. I personally consider these five to be the firm foundation of true leadership, not only in your community activities, but also in your chosen business or profession as well.

1. *Character Is the First Essential Trait.* If you have character, you will instinctively know the difference between right and wrong. Not only will you know the right and proper things to do, but you will also have the courage to do them. You will be a person of honor. You can be trusted. You will not lie, cheat, or steal, no matter what advantage you would gain by doing so.

2. *The Power of Decision Is the Second Essential Trait.* You must be able to make a decision. It is not enough that you use logic and reasoning in making an estimate of the situation. Many people can do that. But only a rare few have the strength of character it takes to make that decision at the right time and then to announce it without fear or hesitation.

What will happen if I do this; what will happen if I do that must always be kept in the back of your mind in making decisions. In essence, the power of decision is simply the vision to see that which needs to be done, and how and when to do it.

3. *The Third Essential Trait Is the Wisdom to Plan and Order.* Once you make your decision about what to do, you must come up with a workable plan to carry it out. Definite and exact tasks must be given to people. Your plan must answer certain specific questions: What is to be done? Who will do it? Where will it be done, when, and how? The wisdom to plan and order is one of the essential traits you will need if you want to lead and master others.

4. *The Courage to Act Is the Fourth Essential Trait of Leadership.* Even though you might have the power of making sound decisions, and of making excellent plans and orders based on those decisions, you will still be far from gaining your goals unless you have the courage to act. The brilliant thinker with the faint heart invites only disaster through his inaction or hesitancy to move. You must have the courage to do what has to be done, despite the costs, the hardships, the hazards, and the sacrifices.

Although you have the vision to see what needs to be done, and the wisdom of Solomon to help you in making those decisions, you won't get the results you're after unless you have the courage to act when immediate action is required.

5. *The Capacity to Manage Is the Final Essential Trait You Need for Leadership.* To be the complete master of others, you must develop the capacity to manage them. The capacity to manage is the systematic approach to the attainment of specific goals. It takes skill and know-how. The management and mastery of people is a tool of good leadership.

It's quite easy to take the perfect combination of abundant and well-trained people-power, all the desired supplies and equipment, unlimited funds, and indefinite time to complete a project. That's no challenge at all. Anyone can do that.

The real challenge to your leadership and your management abilities comes when you have to make the best use of whatever you have on hand to get the job done. You'll be measured by what you get done, not by what you do. It's only the result that counts, not the effort involved.

24

How You Can Be the Center of Attention at Any Party or Other Social Gathering

You can use parties and other social activities to gain power and mastery over people. You don't have to limit your drive for power only to business hours. In fact, a great many times you can get more done at a party than you can at the office. Not only that, but at a party or other social gathering, people tend to let their guard down, especially after they've had a few drinks. That way it'll be much easier for you to influence and control them so you can get what you want.

THE FABULOUS BENEFITS YOU CAN GAIN FROM THIS CHAPTER

1. Parties and social functions give you the perfect opportunity to make important contacts with the right people. You have the chance to socialize with the "power elite" on a one-to-one basis.

2. It's far easier to get a person to say "yes" after he has had a few drinks under his belt. You can get the answer that you want much quicker than you can when you're at the office conducting "official" business.

3. When you use the techniques that I'll give you in this chapter, you'll be able to walk into any group and be as much at ease as if you were home with your own family. You'll be completely comfortable in any social environment.

4. Knowing how to use techniques that will make you the center of attention will help you develop self-confidence and a winning, positive, outgoing personality.

TECHNIQUES YOU CAN USE TO GAIN THESE FABULOUS BENEFITS

How to Best Time Your Arrival for Your Own Benefit

If your boss is the host, show up a couple of minutes early and offer to help. Don't get there too early or he'll still be in the bedroom dressing. I don't mean to imply that you should act like a maid or a butler, but you can offer to help him meet people at the door. That makes you look as if you were the co-host and indicates that you and your boss are really close to each other. People at the office will view you with a great deal more respect the next day.

However, if your intent is to impress the entire group with your arrival, come just a bit late after you're sure that everyone else is there. Then make a dramatic entrance like a conquering hero returning home from the wars. This technique will work for you only if it's a routine party given just for the sake of socializing. It will not work if the party is being given for some VIP. In that case, it's best to arrive a few minutes early and offer your services as I've already mentioned.

How to Make a Dramatic Entrance That Commands Attention

If you want to be the center of attraction at a party or a social event, you must *dare to be different*. I don't mean that you should be so different as to cause people to laugh at you; for example, wearing jeans to a formal dinner. (To get away with that, you have to be so important and famous you don't need to attract attention from anyone.) But my point is that if you dress like everyone else, look like everyone else, and act like everyone else, you'll never be able to stand out from the crowd. Let me give you an example of how to be different and command attention without being obnoxious about it.

Elmer Leterman was one of the most ingenious and successful life insurance salesmen this country has ever seen. He was well known for his interest in the styles of men's clothing. Elmer was constantly experimenting with new ideas without overstepping the boundaries of good taste.

For instance, at a particular award dinner attended by the top business leaders of the entire country, everyone was dressed in formal midnight blue tuxedos with starched white shirts. That is, everyone except Elmer Leterman. When he made his dramatic entrance, all eyes in the ballroom turned to look at him, for he was dressed in a magnificent gray silk formal tuxedo with black satin trim. Although properly dressed, and in perfectly good taste, Elmer was the center of attention simply because he had the courage to be different.

Other Techniques You Can Use to Be the Center of Attention

You can use other methods to be different so you'll be the center of attention wherever you go. Some years ago, I met a young, up-and-coming insurance salesman, Gary Davis, in his company's regional office in Orlando, Florida.

Gary was only five feet, four inches tall. He was a quite common, ordinary looking person except for one thing. He wore a fiery red beard, and this was long before beards were commonplace. "Why?" I asked him.

"To attract attention," Gary said. "I want to make sure that people notice me and remember me. You wear your mustache for the same reason, don't you?"

I had to admit he was right. People remember me as "that man with the salt-and-pepper mustache." If it were not for that, perhaps many of them wouldn't recall the slightly overweight, rather short, middle-aged fellow with thinning hair who wears glasses. Unfortunately, that description fits most American men over forty. But people do remember that man with the "distinguished looking mustache."

Incidentally, that young insurance salesman is now a division manager and assistant vice president of his company. Somebody topside kept him in mind. He still sports that flaming red beard, too.

My point is that you need to be distinctive in some way to be both noticed and remembered. Whatever your most striking physical attribute happens to be, develop it to the fullest, whether it's a beard, a mustache, your eyes, your nose, your legs, whatever. Some famous people used a physical feature, that might be considered a detriment by some, to attract attention. For instance, what would Jimmy Durante have been without his nose or Eddie Cantor without his pop eyes?

One of the best physical attributes you can develop to attract attention is your voice. Your style of talking and the way you converse with others can make a vital contribution to your reputation and your success.

I am fortunate in having a deep, resonant, baritone voice that people remember easily. Two years ago, I saw a lady whom I'd met for just a few brief hours nearly forty years before. "I wouldn't have remembered your face, for then you didn't have a mustache," she said. "But the moment you spoke, I recognized you. Your voice is so distinctive that no one could possibly forget it."

How to Overcome Your Shyness with People

It is normal for a person to be shy and reluctant to strike up a conversation with another person, especially a stranger. So if you feel that way, don't feel badly about it. You are not alone. In fact, you're in darned good company. Seasoned actors and actresses will tell you that they get butterflies in the stomach before going in front of an audience. So do professional speakers.

Gert Behenna, an extremely popular author and lecturer, says that she used to suffer untold agonies before every one of her talks. But gradually, her fear lessened as she kept on speaking until finally she completely overpowered it, simply by doing the thing she was so afraid to do.

So you see, to overcome your shyness of talking with people, you, too, must do the thing you fear to do so you'll have the power to do it. There simply is no other way. This concept applies to everything you do in life. If you want to become a painter, you must paint. If you want to be a writer, you must write. If you want to be an expert swimmer, you must swim. The same point can be made for golf, baseball, selling, music, medicine, and so on. You must make the first move yourself. Until you do that, you'll never gain the power to do anything—and that includes overcoming your shyness of talking with people.

How to Project Your Individuality at a Party

I want to give you a technique here that will not only show you how to project your own individuality at a party, but will also help you overcome your shyness of talking with others at the same time.

One of the major problems of talking with others is that people can't get beyond "How are you?" "How's the wife?" "How's business?" "Beautiful day, isn't it?" If you want to get out of this conversational rut that leads nowhere, overcome your shyness of people, and project your own individuality, all in one fell swoop, then start off with a topic-teaser. Let me give you an example.

I watched a friend of mine, Al J., as he worked this technique to perfection the other night at a social get-together. When he was introduced to an especially gorgeous woman, instead of mumbling, "Hello, how are you, it's nice to meet you," as everyone else had done, he said, "You're really going to be a problem to me tonight!"

Startled at his comment, she asked, "Why do you say that?"

"Because you're so beautiful I'll never be able to take my eyes off you," Al said. "I hope you don't mind."

"Mind?" she asked. "Of course not. How could I mind?"

With just one little sentence, Al was off and running far ahead of the pack.

You can use a topic-teaser to open a conversation. You can arouse interest with it and head off meaningless and boring conversation. Look through your newspaper. I know you can find some interesting topics to discuss rather than the weather, politics, or the state of one's health.

To best project your individuality and to make sure you're on safe ground, choose a topic in which you're well versed so you won't get caught short. Avoid controversial subjects that can create enemies for you. Abortion, for example, is hardly a subject for parties or social gatherings. No matter which side you choose, you'll be in trouble. If you're for abortion, some will view you as a person who advocates murder. If you're against abortion, others will view you as being out of touch with reality. Either way, you'll lose, so don't use such controversial subjects for topic-teasers. Of course, you do want a subject that's interesting enough to stimulate a spirited conversation, but not one that creates enemies and hard feelings.

Still Other Methods You Can Use
to Command Attention

I've already mentioned personal appearance, clothing, and your conversational ability as ways of attracting attention. But there are still some other methods you can use, and I'd like to give you a few examples. Always keep in mind that *color and movement* are two important aspects of attracting attention and holding it. That's why in most TV commercials you see today, the person making the sales pitch never stands still. He keeps moving constantly so your eyes are forced to follow him.

If you can do any magic tricks, you can use these two principles of color and movement to attract and hold everyone's attention. You don't have to make rabbits or doves appear and disappear from your hat, or saw a woman in half. I well remember a sergeant I met in the army who was an amateur magician. He was constantly in demand to perform at parties. He entertained at both NCO clubs and Officers' Clubs and made a small fortune doing so.

His two major feats of legerdemain were done with Ping-Pong balls and cards. People were absolutely fascinated by his tricks with Ping-Pong balls. He would make them appear and disappear from his mouth, his ear, his nose, behind the back of his hand, and so on. I've watched him dozens of times put six or eight Ping-Pong balls in his mouth one at a time and then open his mouth to show they were no longer there. He also had a variety of card tricks he used that kept his audience both baffled and spellbound.

I used to be able to snap quarters and half-dollars up my coat sleeve with my fingers and then pull them out from behind a person's ear until arthritis caught up with me and my fingers got too stiff. You lose your audience in a hurry when the quarters fall on the floor!

My father-in-law had a clever trick in which a marked dime that he put in his pocket ended up inside a tiny cloth sack inside a small matchbox that was wrapped with several rubber bands. The secret of this trick was a flattened metal Tums tube that was inserted beforehand through the matchbox edges and into the mouth of the small sack. The dime slid down the tube which was then withdrawn from the matchbox and kept in his pocket, of course.

Then he would take the matchbox bound with rubber bands

out of his pocket and hand it to the person so he could recover his marked dime. I don't know if the Tums people still put their product in a metal tube or not. If not, and you want to use this trick, I'm sure you can find a suitable substitute at your local magic store. If you have no stores that specialize in magic where you live, ask your local library to give you the names and addresses of mail order companies that do.

Simple card tricks that are easy to do can still attract and baffle an audience. Not only can you gain and hold people's attention, but you can also have a lot of good fun at the same time. And if you get good enough with your magic tricks, you'll find that you have more party invitations than you can begin to handle.

A "Party Map" That Shows You Where to Stand for Maximum Power

The first thing to remember is that powerful people rarely sit down at a party. Not only does this indicate fatigue and a general lack of energy, but it also prevents movement and puts the person sitting down at a disadvantage because he has to look up to carry on a conversation.

Always stand where the power brokers stand. This is usually at either end of the bar. This position is most advantageous for several reasons. A person can stand with his back to the wall and survey the entire room. He can place an elbow or an arm on the bar and rest without actually appearing to do so.

He can glance down the bar and watch the heavy drinkers, making a mental note of those who can't seem to handle their liquor. The conclusion usually drawn about a person who can't handle alcohol well is that he can't handle himself or any important business matters either.

The power person can also get another drink from the bartender easily without having to navigate the entire room to refill his glass. Too many trips to the bar from across the room can easily attract the wrong kind of attention.

Some power players prefer to stand in a corner of the room waiting for people to come to them. I do not recommend this for a variety of reasons. First of all, it's simply too difficult to get out of the corner to get a drink from the bar without being obvious about it. Second, it's all too easy to get boxed in by those with less power who surround you. But if you stand at either end of the bar, sooner or later everyone at the party will drift there to refill an empty glass. They can't help but notice you and pay attention to you.

If you don't drink alcoholic beverages yourself, so much the better. You can drink cola, ginger ale, even water, and no one except you and the bartender will know the difference. For many years now I've gone to parties, stood at the end of the bar, and consumed gallons of Horse's Necks, the name for a nonalcoholic drink that looks for all the world like a Tom Collins.

I've been admired time and again by the people who really count for my ability to handle liquor at a party. Only the bartender and I know what's actually in my glass. It's amazing how much more you can learn about people at a party when you don't drink.

25

How to Hold and Increase Your Power and Mastery over People Year After Year

Your knowledge about how to gain power and mastery over people is at this point basically complete. You now have all the information you need to achieve power, influence, and control over others. From now on, it's a matter of consolidating your gains and being prepared to expand your influence in an ever wider and larger area.

In each chapter of this book, I've given you certain specific benefits that can be yours when you gain power and mastery over people. I would now like to review and recap some of those benefits that will come your way when you hold and increase your power over others year after year.

I want to do this here because I know from past experience that people tend to feel they have it made at this point so they let down and take it easy. But if you want to be successful, you cannot do that. I know when you reread these benefits, you'll be inspired and motivated to persist in your drive to gain power and mastery over people.

THE WONDERFUL BENEFITS YOU CAN GAIN FROM THE MASTERY OF PEOPLE

1. When you know how to master people, you'll gain great power over them. You can have them provide you with everything you want in life. You'll become a leader of people; not just a convincing persuader or a clever manipulator, but a true leader of

253

others, pure and simple. Virtually anything that you ask, others will now have to give to you.

2. When you use the techniques I've given you to gain mastery over people, you'll attain a degree of personal power greater than anything you've ever experienced before. Prestige, respect, influence, all these can be yours now. Even formerly unfriendly people will come to you—actually want to be with you—to do things for you.

3. You'll be able to master the most powerful people: the tough bosses, obstinate customers and clients, stubborn authorities, and anyone else who's been holding you back from the big money and success that are rightfully yours. They'll be like putty in your hands now.

4. Perhaps, up to now, your search for friends and companions has been fruitless. It could be that people were unresponsive to you because you didn't know how to approach them. Or perhaps you haven't been able to find anyone worthy of your attention. If you read just one chapter a day, in less than a month you'll know how to make these problems disappear. In fact, about the only problem you'll have from now on is handling all the people who'll be attracted to you.

5. When you gain mastery over people, you can be the leader in all the social, business, political, and neighborhood matters in which you participate. You can easily be elected to the presidency and chairmanship of clubs and groups as a result of your power, influence, and control over others. Wherever you go, you'll be hailed and recognized as a leader of people.

6. The mastery of people will open the door to an amazing development: the emergence of a brand-new you. Your true individuality (possibly repressed for many years)—the real you—will now begin to surface. This new you will be different in looks, manner, speech, poise, confidence, bearing, and most important of all, *power*.

With this new power of yours, you won't have to worry about your education or the way you speak. You'll be able to act correctly in any social environment. You can walk into any group anywhere and be as much at ease and as comfortable as if you were home with your own family.

7. This new personality will begin to pay off for you immediately. For instance, you'll see how you'll be able to speak your mind in a way that everyone wants to, but nobody has the courage to. Perhaps there are many things you've been wanting to speak up about, but you've been hesitant about it before. Now you'll have what it takes to stand up before a group, a crowd, yes, even an unruly mob and put them entirely under your complete control. You can be the leader of any neighborhood, religious, civic, fraternal, business, or political group you want.

8. Your power at this point will become self-generating. It will actually start multiplying of its own accord. You'll find that your great new personality will act like a magnet drawing people to you. This personal magnetism and charisma will grow and grow. Others will not only agree with you, but they'll also actually help you get whatever you want.

9. Important people will start coming to you, offering you business deals, social honors, positions of leadership and respect, perhaps even that big job or position you've always wanted. So, aim for the top; you can make it. Has chairman of the board or owning your own business been your dream? Maybe you'd prefer an important executive position with a big corporation. It makes no difference. You now have the power techniques you need to be an outstanding success in business, wherever you choose to be.

10. If you're having trouble with your marriage, or having other romantic problems, you can now forget them. With your new magnetic personality, it's possible for you to have the appeal of a movie star and the charm of a diplomat. Even if you feel that you've been cheated out of a truly great romance, don't worry. It's not too late even now, for a brand-new irresistible you has just emerged from that former passive shell of yours.

11. If you will look in the mirror you'll see a completely new person, a person with new talents, power, and influence who commands respect wherever he or she goes—a person who gets everything he or she wants. That person is you, and you can now enjoy to the fullest your new important look, your new manner-isms, your new walk and bearing, your new charm, your whole new station in life. I know it seems like a miracle, but it's true. You are not the same person at all who started reading this book, *25 Steps to*

Power and Mastery over People, a short time ago. You've undergone a wonderful transformation, so enjoy it to the fullest. It's all yours.

As I told you, I wanted to emphasize these wonderful benefits to you again in this chapter, for from my past experience, I know that people can feel they have it made and that they can sit down and rest on their laurels. But that is not true. You must keep working to stay at the top.

TECHNIQUES YOU CAN USE TO RETAIN THESE BENEFITS

Your Key to Total Victory Is Your Follow-Through

The young bowler seemed to do everything just right in his approach. He stepped off with the proper foot. He did not drift from side to side on his way to the foul line; nor did he allow his eyes to stray from their target. He released the ball smoothly and watched it roll down the lane to break smartly into the 1-3 pocket just at the right moment, only to leave the 5-pin standing. What happened? What went wrong? Why didn't he get a strike?

"Your ball had no strength," his instructor said. "It had no power because you quit before the job was done. *You didn't follow through!*"

The same remark is made every day of the week by golf instructors, baseball and football coaches, executives and managers, foremen and supervisors in business and industry.

"*You failed because you didn't follow through!*"

To keep that from happening to you, follow these two techniques:

1. *Exploit Your Initial Success to the Fullest.* In war, the final victory will go to the commander who has the ability and the foresight to follow up his initial advantage. Once the line has been breached and the enemy turns toward the rear, the opportunity has come to completely eliminate him. A confused enemy in disorganized retreat is an easy mark for a swift and determined pursuit.

In business, the same idea holds true. When you've sold him the suit, don't stop there. Follow through and sell him the shoes, socks, tie, shirt, and hat to go with the suit.

The biggest profits in the automobile industry aren't made when the car is sold. They're made when the sharp salesman follows through and gets the customer to buy all those plush optional extras, from the stereo tape player and FM radio with front and rear speakers to the push-button-controlled power antenna.

This idea of following through applies not only to business, but also to the mastery of people. You can exploit your initial success and insure a complete victory if you will *follow through with the utmost energy*.

2. *Insure Your Continued Success*. If you've developed your resources and made ready for the long haul ahead, you'll have sufficient reserve strength to follow through and insure your continued success.

For instance, young musical groups come and go constantly. Out of every 100, only one or two at the most will still be around a year after they've started. Why? Well, as a popular night show host once said, "They don't have more than a few numbers they can do for an audience. They sound terrific for the first four or five songs, but after that, they're dead. They can't get past the second encore."

You can avoid that death trap if you'll develop your follow-through to insure your continued success. To do that, you'll need to make an extra effort and be persistent above all else.

Remember How You Got Where You Are Today

Don't become complacent and think you've got it made when you're on the top of the heap. You must always keep in mind the fourteen basic needs and desires that all people have. Continue to be aware of your followers' needs, keep fulfilling those needs so they will always get what they want, and your position of leadership and mastery over others will be secure.

Politicians are voted out of office when they become so filled with self-importance that they forget the needs of their constituents. But the smart ones who continue to fulfill the needs of the voters in their state or district are elected time and again until politics becomes their sole career. For example, when you say Congressman in Florida, people automatically say Claude Pepper the same way they say Coke when you mention a soft drink.

How to Set Up a "Lifetime Power Plan" to Project Your Goals for Those Years Ahead

I've seen a lot of plans for successful achievement over the years, but the one I feel is the most outstanding comes from Paul J. Meyer, President of SMI International, Inc. An expert in inspiring people to give it their best shot, Mr. Meyer calls his formula the...

MILLION-DOLLAR PERSONAL SUCCESS PLAN*

1. *Crystallize Your Thinking.* Determine what specific goal you want to achieve. Then dedicate yourself to its attainment with unswerving singleness of purpose, the trenchant zeal of a crusader.

2. *Develop a Plan for Achieving Your Goal,* and a deadline for its attainment. Plan your progress carefully: hour-by-hour, day-by-day, month-by-month. Organized activity and maintained enthusiasm are the well-springs of your power.

3. *Develop a Sincere Desire for the Things You Want in Life.* A burning desire is the greatest motivator of every human action. The desire for success implants "success consciousness" which in turn, creates a vigorous and ever-increasing "habit of success."

4. *Develop Supreme Confidence in Yourself and Your Own Abilities.* Enter every activity without giving mental recognition to the possibility of defeat. Concentrate on your strengths, instead of your weaknesses...on your powers, instead of your problems.

5. *Develop a Dogged Determination to Follow Through on Your Plan,* regardless of obstacles, criticism or circumstances or what other people say, think, or do. Construct your determination with sustained effort, controlled attention, and concentrated energy. Opportunities never come to those who wait...they are captured by those who dare to attack.

The One Character Trait You'll Need for the Long Haul

The one major success factor that separates the men from the boys and the women from the girls is *perseverance*. It's easy to be

---

*Reprinted by permission of Paul J. Meyer, President of SMI International, Inc., of Waco, Texas. All rights reserved. Copyright 1962.

full of fire and perseverance about a project when everything's going all right. It's a tough proposition to handle when it starts raining inside! That's when the boys and girls quit and the men and women keep right on going.

Without perseverance, you have no hope of success. Perseverance means to hold out, to last, to continue, to remain steadfast. Perseverance is the ability to put up with pain, pressure, fatigue, and distress. People who make it to the top have one character trait in common—perseverance.

One of our famous presidents described perseverance in effect this way: "Nothing in the world can take the place of perseverance. Talent will not; nothing is more comman than unsuccessful men with talent. Genius will not; the world is full of educated derelicts. Perseverance and determination alone are omnipotent. The slogan 'Press on!' has solved and will always solve the problems of the human race."

That's the kind of perseverance you will need, not only to master people, but also to retain your power over them. Nothing else will ever do.

How to Get the Most Out of This Book

You cannot possibly retain all the valuable information in this book with only one reading. After all, it's taken me a lifetime to collect the material that's gone into it. You should read it and reread it until its principles and techniques have become second nature and are a living part of you.

Rather than read it from cover to cover again and again as some people do when they make a project out of reading the Bible once a year, do it this way. If you are having a particular problem that you need an answer to, find the appropriate chapter and read it before going to bed. Then sleep on it. Nine times out of ten, the answer will come to you crystal clear in the morning. If it does not, read it again and again until you do get your answer. Let me give you some examples so I can better show you exactly what I mean:

First of all, I would recommend that you type up a list of the fourteen secret motivators that everybody has and slip it under the glass on your desk or place it somewhere so you can see it at all times. Remember, to fulfill a person's basic needs and desires is the key to your mastery over people. You can always use this knowledge to gain power, influence, and control over others.

Let's suppose you're having a problem with getting people to listen to you. Go back and reread Chapter 2, "How to Get People to Pay Attention to You." Review the techniques that are in this chapter, use them, and you're bound to be successful.

No matter whether it's a matter of building up your self-confidence, giving commands that will always be obeyed without question, getting people to back you to the hilt, developing the "aura of command" that makes others give way to you immediately, building an army of loyal followers, or some other problem that's bothering you, you can find the answers that will help you when you refresh your memory by reading the appropriate chapter again.

Why am I so sure that this program of *25 Steps to Power and Mastery over People* will work for you? Because I've already seen it work for thousands of others. Yes, it's true. Thousands of people have already attained mastery over people with this powerful yet virtually effortless program. They were just common and ordinary people at the beginning. But by the time they finished the program—after spending only a few minutes a day for twenty-five days—in less than a month they became vastly more powerful than they ever dreamed possible before. And if all those people could do it, then so can you.

Index